TEMPUS
Oral History
SERIES

SOUTH SHIELDS
voices

Mrs George Smith of No. 15, Oxford Street with her children in 1919. Left to right: Mary, Matthew, John and Annie. With his wife, Florence, Matthew went on to run M.H. Smith newsagents at No. 85 Mortimer Road from 1934 until they retired in 1974.

TEMPUS
Oral History
SERIES

SOUTH SHIELDS
voices

Compiled by
John Carlson and Joyce Carlson

TEMPUS

First published 1997, reprinted 1999
Copyright © John Carlson and Joyce Carlson, 1997

Tempus Publishing Limited
The Mill, Brimscombe Port,
Stroud, Gloucestershire, GL5 2QG

ISBN 0 7524 1065 2

Typesetting and origination by
Tempus Publishing Limited
Printed in Great Britain by
Midway Clark Printing, Wiltshire

NCB railway staff outside Westoe Colliery Shed in 1964. Inside the cab is electrical engineer Fred Bond. Back row: electrician's mate Albert Parker, fitter Brian Martin, blacksmith's striker Matt O'Connell, electricians mate D. Fowler and blacksmith G. Liscombe. Front row: apprentice electrician Steve McLaren, time clerk (unknown) and railway guard Bobby Simms. The locomotive (No. 2) dates from 1908 and was constructed in Munich.

CONTENTS

Bugler M.R. Charlton and bugler A. David of the Durham Light Infantry in France during the First World War. They appear to be posed in front of a photographic backdrop shortly after arriving in France.

Fowler Street around 1920. (Courtesy Beamish the North of England Open Air Museum.)

INTRODUCTION

The text of this book is made up entirely of the memories of South Shields people and covers events in the town from around 1910 to the mid 1980s. Around thirty-five people were interviewed between September 1996 to June 1997; ranging from a river diver, an ice cream maker, a bus inspector, a ballet teacher, a riveter and a TV comedy performer and scriptwriter. Almost all have nothing in common except they have lived in Shields for most of their lives. Their reminiscences cover time spent at school, their days at work and how life went on during the war. More personal memories include, the thrill of moving into a new house, swimming from the pier and placing a first bet with an illegal bookie.

The people interviewed are not presented as a cross section of South Shields people. They are sometimes people personally known to the compilers, sometimes they were recommended to us by friends and sometimes they just suggested themselves. Neither are their stories to be taken as a definitive history of the town. Rather this is a set of reminiscences, a list of events that stand out as significant in a personal history.

Most of these interviews have been carried out in the participants own homes and often started with the preamble, 'There's nothing I can really tell you about Shields.' Then after a few minutes the memories came flooding back, the family albums would be produced and another cassette tape would have to be found for the recorder. These interviews have been transcribed from the recordings almost word for word with only the minimum of editing. As with any project of this sort, recollections can differ and where discrepancies have arisen, the compilers have let both versions stand.

7

GROUP BY W. H. WARREN **HARTON COLLIERY BAND. SOUTH SHIELDS.** *SOUTH SA*
THE CHAMPION BAND OF GREAT BRITAIN FOR 1919. WINNERS OF THE GREAT BELLE VUE CONTEST. MANCHESTER. SEPTEMBER 1st, 1919.

ACKNOWLEDGEMENTS

For sharing their stories, or loaning their photographs, I would like to thank, Hugh Amess, Edith Atkinson, Geordie Atkinson, Colin Barnsley, David Barnsley, Ken Barnsley, Maisie Bell, Alfred Beris, Kathleen Burdon, Shiela Burrows, Olga Carlson, Ken Carter, Jean Cockayne, Ken Corner, Tom Dawson, Ethel Dawson, Dave Ditchburn, Reta Emery, Evelyn Drew, Malcom Grady, Bill Hatcher, Bob Hedley, Bill Henderson jnr, Bill Henderson snr, Jean Henderson, John Irwin, Ernie Keedy, Terry Killen, John Landells, Isabella Myers, Michael Minchella, Harry Peasland, Mary Peterson, Eddie Post, Bill Salkeld, M.S. Shabilla, Jean Shanahan, Matty Smith, Jim Thompson, Jack Thorpe, John Tinmouth, Dolly Taws, John Weir and Raymond Wilkinson.

I would like to thank Keith Bardwell of South Tyneside Libraries, Beamish the North of England Open Air Museum, Tyne and Wear Archive Service, Newcastle City Library and the *Shields Gazette* for providing other photographs.

Finally I would also like to thank my father Charles Carlson, Kevin Bashford, Andrew Clark, Sandrine Dalban, Dan Entwisle, Thomas Gitopoulos, Howard Goldsbrough, Shirley Mei-jung Huang, Alice King, Stephen Roddam, Stuart Smith, Neil Tweddle and all South Shields people of goodwill everywhere.

John Carlson
South Shields
September 1997

CHAPTER 1

First Impressions

Spring comes to the South Marine Park in the 1930s.

Ships approaching The Groyne around 1910. Construction work on the River Drive is taking place in the foreground. The railway in the middle ground is the Tyne Improvement Commission's line to the limestone Quarry at Trow Rocks. (Courtesy South Tyneside Libraries)

Light

When I was two, I hated to be in the dark. I lived in a flat with a gas light and I didn't like flame either, but of course there had to be a match struck to get the light going. One day some men came to our flat and they worked all day. They were there for quite some time and I was told to behave myself. When they had gone my dad lifted me up and said, 'Press that switch.' There was a round switch on the wall. It was gold and there was a little black lever in the middle and he wanted me to press it. All of a sudden it was light! It was beautiful and glowing. The whole room was filled and he said, 'Now we've got electric, that's electric light.' For weeks afterwards we went around telling people, 'We've got the electric now.'

Isabella Myers

Strange Stamps

My father and most of my family went to sea and we were always getting postcards and letters with strange stamps on. I would be taken to The Groyne to see the ships coming in and to watch for my father.

Jean Shanahan

The Ice Cream Business

Both sides of my family have always been in the ice cream business. My grandfather, Giuseppe Minchella, known as Joe, came over from San Michele in Italy when he was in his mid-teens. He was married to a girl called Maria Capaldi. Shortly after arriving in the area he set up in the ice cream business. My other grandfather, Fred, never really learned to speak English properly. His name was Alfreido and I can imagine him trying to say his name at the registry office, 'Alfreido, Alfffrrreido', and the officials ending up writing down Fred. My father's name was Antonio and that would come out on official documents as Tony. Giuseppe came out as Joseph and strangely enough his wife was called Mary.

Michael Minchella

High Road Bank

When I was six or seven, when the High Road bank was covered in ice, I used to borrow my dad's pit shoes, the ones with the steel caps on, and go sledging. With just one push from a mate, I was straight down the bank. It was like being on a skateboard. When I was about ten, my dad made a barrow for me. The wheels were off one of the trucks that they used to push down the pit and I could be heard coming from miles off. Sometimes I would fill this barrow full of coal and push it right down to James Mather Street off Ocean Road and then to my aunt's in St Vincent's Street. She used to give me money for sweets to eat on the way back.

Bill Salkeld

Honour Bound

In the 1920s the young girls of Shields could resort to rather frightening methods to get themselves good husbands. In those days it didn't take too much to go on between two people to constitute a proposal of marriage. An engagement would be considered in court as a legally binding proposal, even a few letters would sometimes count as a firm intention, and the men were honour bound to fulfil a proposal. The girls would go out with the young seafaring apprentices two or three times and then, when he went away to sea, her parents would get going on the matrimonial prospects. They would approach the ship owning firms to see when his ship was coming back and sometimes the whole family would be waiting at the quay side when he returned. If the girls managed to put a foot on deck, then the men would be almost duty bound to marry them. My mother-in-law was engaged to a young officer. He had been an orphan and was practically brought up on a ship (*Wellesley*) that people used to call, 'The Bad Boy's Ship.' It was permanently moored by the Tyne and the name was quite erroneous because they were all good boys really. He had his seafaring certificates by the time he met my mother-in-law and her aunt approved of him. While he was away to India, she was out walking with a friend who introduced her to the man who was to

The Training Ship *Wellesley*, moored off North Shields. (Courtesy South Tyneside Libraries.)

become her husband. He was at the Marine School in Ocean Road taking a master's ticket and when the other men found out he was going out with another man's girl he became the butt of jokes and quite a bit of shame because the seafarers didn't like to see another of their number hoodwinked. So he went to the aunt and said that he had been going out with the daughter and either the girl should become engaged to him or he would not darken their doorstep again. Upon which the aunt seized her chance and the two of them got married. When the first young man came home from India he took it all very well. On the rebound he met a young girl of sixteen who went out with him a few times. Later, when his ship docked in Wales, she was there waiting for him and managed to get aboard, demanded marriage and of course he

was duty bound to marry her. That kind of thing went on a lot in Shields because seafaring men were usually considered to be a good catch for a single woman.

Jean Shanahan

On the Beach

Every night, straight from school, we used to go down to the beach to bathe. On the way down we crossed the Marsden Rattler and passed a little hut beside the Leas that belonged to the manager of the Palace. I can't remember his name, but he always wore a trilby. You could buy long strips of hanky panky toffee there, they were half an inch wide and you could hang it around your neck. Then we would pass a

The path down to Trow Rocks in the early 1930s. (Courtesy South Tyneside Libraries.)

wooden bungalow where an old lady lived. She was a bit of an animal lover and she would often leave water out for the dogs. We went to the patch of sand just beside the pier where the coast guard post is and we would run about with nothing on. You wouldn't do that now, you wouldn't get parents letting their kids do it today.

Ernie Keedy

Loads Of Heat

In our flat in Marshall Wallis Road we had an old iron open range fireplace. It gave off loads of heat and the oven had these hot plates inside which we used at night to warm the bed. They were great, but you always had to get them out of the bed before you fell asleep or when you woke up the bed would be freezing. My

dad used to come home from sea with ingots of lead and we used to spend hours melting it down and pouring it into toy soldier moulds. Today you wouldn't even be allowed to touch the lead.

Malcolm Grady

Marbles In The Gutters

We used to play marbles in the gutters all the way home from school. There was no such thing as hygiene then.

Ernie Keedy

Into The Fields

We used to go out into the fields and eat privet and suck clover

13

A South Shields Corporation tram, displaying adverts for local charities, at the Dean Road Depot. (Courtesy South Tyneside Libraries.)

and people would call it eating bread and cheese. It tasted horrible and it was un-hygienic but we still used to do it.

Ethel Dawson

Shoeless

A charity show I used to appear in quite often was known and publicised as 'The Shoeless Children's Fund.' Now if that isn't a reflection of the thirties, tell me what is.

Bob Hedley

Police Shoes

If you were poor, then you used to get the police shoes. Everyone at school knew it was disgrace to get them. If I had qualified for them, I think I would have rather have gone out with bare feet. Some children would get tickets for free school dinners. It was awful really the way they marked people out if they were receiving welfare. You would think children had no sensitivity because they would be made to stand in a line at one end of the room and the ones that paid would be standing at the other. The teachers didn't seem to realise that they would just curl up inside when that used

14

to happen.

Mary Peterson

The shoes I got from the police station were men's brogues and they had two holes punched in the side so you couldn't take them to the pawn shop and sell them. At least that was the theory. The police took my old shoes and I had to walk in the new ones all the way home from Kepple Street to Canterbury Street. When I got as far as Hartington Terrace my feet hurt so much I took the shoes off and walked the rest of the way in my bare feet. When I got home I was crying and there were great big blisters right across my feet. My dad was so annoyed he took the police shoes off me and flung them to the back of the fire. The next morning he went out and bought me a pair of sand shoes

Olga Carlson

A Bread Knife In His Hand

One day the girl on the other side of the street invited me into her house. I had played out with her quite a few times before, but I had never seen her father around. That day she told me that he was home from hospital and asked if I wanted to see him. We went to her house and were playing in her back living room when her father came in and said hello, but he had a bread knife in his hand. Then he started to chase us around the table wielding the bread knife and shouting and baring his teeth. My friend and I screamed like mad. After a few times around the table

Bill Corner stands outside his house in Talbot Road. The girl is Lissie – Ken Corner's aunt.

I managed to get away and ran out of the door, down the stairs and out of the house yelling for my mother. That was the first and only time I saw her father.

Joyce Carlson

A Visit From The Dentist

When I was very young we lived next door to my grandma and my Aunt Lissie in one of the new houses in Harton Lane. One day they both came into our house and helped my mam put a blanket and a white sheet on the big wooden table in the back room that posh people called the dining room.

15

Someone told me that the dentist was coming to the house. They had just finished re-arranging the furniture when there was a knock at the front door. A man came in carrying a brown leather suitcase which he put down on a little table they had brought in from the out house. He took a white coat out of the case, put it on and told my mam to lie on the big table. Aunt Lissie took me out of the room and left grandma with mam. The next time I saw mam she had had her teeth out.

Ken Corner

Settees And Sideboards

My father was a sea captain on Norwegian sailing ships. There were six of us children and my mother had a servant. My mother died when I was seven and my father left the sea to look after his family. He didn't get the dole because he was three stamps short so life was pretty bleak for the seven of us. Before the war my uncle in Norway used to send us an allowance once a month. My brother used to have to cycle up to Newcastle and get the cheque changed into pounds because the shops in Shields charged too much. It was a big day when the cheque came and us kids would get a penny each. My brother Tom and I used to spend ours at the corner shop, a ha'peth of this and a ha'peth of that. Tom used to like Silver Links but they were dear and we didn't get many for a penny. I used to buy Minty Bullets and Aniseed Balls.

We had very little furniture. I used to go to my friends' houses and see settees and sideboards. Then I would ask my father, 'How come we don't have anything like that?' He told me he had to cut everything up and burn it to keep the fire going during the general strike because we hadn't any coal. There was an old catalogue in the house and my brother Tom and I used to look at that and say to each other, 'If I had a lot of money that's what I would get.' We used to take a page each and pick out the things we would have. Later I would cut pictures out to make furniture for my dolls house.

We didn't have a toilet. We did have an outside one but we couldn't afford the water rate and we had to have the water cut off. We had to use the neighbours.

Olga Carlson

Coal Bricks

My mates who had fathers out of work used to help them make coal bricks. We would go to the Downhill tip and collect coal dust. You could see the fellers with their bags on their backs wheeling the dust home. They made the bricks in a little wooden mould, mostly from cement and coal duff. When you put them on the fire they never gave a bright flame but they got very hot.

Ernie Keedy

Hard To Come By

During the miners disputes in the 1970s, coal was very hard to come by. One Sunday afternoon, in late November, I walked up to the ground

The last days. Only one of Tyne Docks Arches remains in use in this 1968 view. (Courtesy Beamish Museum)

that had been the coal wagon sidings for Tyne Dock arches. The arches were shut and the sidings pulled up. Over the years tons of coal must have dropped out of the wagons. In the half dark I could see hundreds of people scattered across the ground, crouched over and scooping up the coal with their hands and small shovels and carrying it away in Hinton's and Fine Fayre plastic bags. Someone filled the back of a Morris Minor with coal until it was right down on the back axle then it struggled away with its wheels churning against the ballast. It was a strange sight, but I suppose many people still had coal fires and they had nothing else to burn.

Jerimia Cornelius

A New House

When I was very young we lived at 122, Back Frederick Street. We always had to say Back Frederick Street when we gave our address. About 1924 we got a council house at the Ridgeway at Park Avenue beside the White Ensign. I remember mam taking me up there on a rattling tramcar. She had a brand new broom and a brand new bucket and when we got in there wasn't any electricity because it wasn't connected up yet. But there was water and we were provided with hurricane lamps until they got the power hooked up. Everybody in the family rejoiced because we had a bath and everything. And then came the 1926 strike and we couldn't pay the rent and we had to

17

Hugh Amess in his garden at Palm Avenue on the Cleadon Park Estate in 1959.

move back into town again. In fact some of the miners were actually paying off rent arrears of about six pence a week when the strike was over.

Bob Hedley

We Certainly Felt Quite Lucky!

When I was born the Hyde Street flat became too small for our family so we moved to the Cleadon Park Estate which had just been built. The houses had inside baths and all the modern facilities of the day. Most people at that time had outdoor toilets and had to carry water into the house and boil it, so we certainly felt quite lucky. We had very large back gardens and with my friends, Edith and Margaret, we played out there with our dolls and skipping ropes. Edith used to dress up her kitten as a baby and would take it out for a walk in her pram. We walked along the top of the wooden fence between the gardens, pretending we were on a tight rope. We had an old air raid shelter in the garden which was covered in moss and we loved to climb on the top of it. Sometimes we used to stage little concerts in our back garden. This was before I had been to dancing classes and we just used to make the show up as we went along. Sometimes my mother would make us chips and bring a plate of them out for us.

Kathleen Burdon

My Grandmother's Buck Eye And Golden Pheasant.

I was always a little bit frightened of my grandmother because she looked like some wild gypsy. She had long black

18

hair and claw like hands and she used to cover them in Vaseline and then scrape it back across her hair. She would sit like Queen Victoria in a black rocking chair wearing a black shawl and as soon as I went in it was, 'You have to go to the shops, I want two ounces of Buck Eye if they haven't got that get two ounces of Golden Pheasant.' I hated going to the shops for her because I used to hate asking for snuff. She used to take so much I think she might have been addicted to it.

Mary Peterson

Newly-married Bob Hanrahan and Jenny Wilkinson outside their new house on the Cleadon Park estate, c. 1941.

Morning Swim

My mother and I used to go to the open air swimming baths at the beach very early in the morning. She used to insist that this was the only time in which it was clean. We used to be there at six o'clock. I used to dip my toe in and that was enough for me, but my mother was quite a strong swimmer and she used to take part in swimming galas between the ferry landing on the south pier and the foreshore. My father walked the length of the pier each day and he said he would see the same people day after day swimming from it and the beach. People used to believe

Standing: Evelyn Johnson, Ken Barnsley, Florrie Squires, Dora Barsted, Sarah Raine. Seated: Frank Raine, Betty Wilkinson, Jenny Barsted. They are in the back garden of No. 18, Colin Avenue, Sutton Trust Estate, 1957.

The open air swimming pool on the foreshaw. (Courtesy South Tyneside Libraries)

that sea water did you good and some of the women swimmers would claim they never suffered from arthritis.

John Irwin

In The Back Lane

Sometimes I would look out the window and there would be a man with a white muffler, a cap and far from good clothing walking very slowly up the lane with his cap held out in front of him. He would be willing to tap dance or sing a song to try to make some money. One man came around with a cane mat and he would play spoons and tap dance. There was a paint tin top held on his shoes by one nail that would make a marvellous sound as it clattered against the cobbles.

Bob Hedley

A man used to come around our back lane singing from the back of his throat with his cap outstretched in his hands. He was always half drunk and we used to open the window and throw him a penny just to get rid of him.

Olga Carlson

When we lived on the Law Top, the fisher women used to come around the lanes carrying fish on their backs in big baskets called keel. They came over from North Shields fish quay on the low ferry which ran from the landing at North Shields to a landing in South Shields down the bank from the end of Mile End Road. They used to sell their fresh herring for twelve a penny. My mother used to send me out into the lane to buy from them, but she would say to me first, 'Get twelve herring and ask for one for yourself, but when you ask for that, don't forget to say please.' Like a good little girl I used to go out and say, 'Twelve fresh herring and one for myself please', and I used to get thirteen and just had to pay for twelve.

Isabella Myers

A woman we called Whiskey Belly used to sell props in the back lane. She smoked a pipe and if the kids made fun of her she used to swear back at them like a trooper. When the coal men came around you used to have to shout, 'Hey Misses the coal man is coming', so the women could let the prop down or the sheets would all turn black. Someone used to come around selling vinegar from a barrel on a cart. Then there would be the fish people. They would go to the quay, buy a box of herring, hire a hand cart from Hanrattey's in Laygate or Fenwicks in Bewick Street for about sixpence a day, and go around the back lane selling herring at twelve a penny. You would find stinking fish boxes lying in the back lane because when they had sold their load all they wanted to do was take the barrow back to Hanrattey's. I can never forget the filthy back lanes with the dead cats and the dogs' dirt and the cobble stones. They were so dirty we used to have to rub the cats feet with butter to get the tar off. At the bottom of our back lane, on the corner

The 'low' or 'penny' ferry. St Steven's church spire can be seen in the background. (Courtesy South Tyneside Libraries)

Colin Barnsley aged four on the North Beach.

of Imeary Street and George Potts Street, there was Gregory's the coach builders. There was a gable end to the building and we used to watch the men mending the wagons. My dad was a business man so we had a bath in the house. We were posh, but I don't think we had hot water.

Ernie Keedy

Hot Sand Bottle

My father used to fill a long stone hot water bottle with sand to retain the heat then he would put it in the oven to warm it up. The first one off to bed got the bottle. By the time I went I got the oven shelf with an old towel rapped around it, but it used to keep me warm.

Olga Carlson

Three Times Under

My earliest memories are so dramatic that they live with me to this day. I was about four. My parents lived in Wouldhave Street which ran parallel to Seafield Terrace and I spent a lot of time playing close to the park lake. One day we were sailing our boats then the next thing I knew I was in the water. Then just as suddenly I was being pulled out by big hands and told to get myself home. Shortly afterwards I was in the park, again playing close to the waterfall beside the band stand. I can remember falling into the green water and sinking downwards and coming back towards the surface when I saw this hand coming thorough the water, grabbing hold of me and pulling me out. I still dream about that water and a hand coming towards me. Then about a year later I was on Littlehaven beach. At that time there used to be a lot of pleasure boats sailing out from there, taking people out for runs in the harbour. I was playing in the water and for some reason I decided to hang on to one of the ropes that hung down from the back of the boat. Then suddenly it shot out into the water with me hanging on behind. One of the men on the boat shouted at me to let go which I did, but by this time I was out in deep water and as soon as I let go I was floundering. Then a man came out to save me. As a result of those incidents I still have nightmares and I still can't swim a stroke to save my life.

Colin Barnsley

Going For Messages

When I was eleven there was a woman living opposite us who had diabetes. She had to have special bread and on a Saturday morning she asked me to go to Northcote Street to pick it up. When I got back I thought that would be it, but she gave me another note and told me to stand in the fruit shop queue. Then when I had brought them back, she asked me to go somewhere else. There was always a queue at each shop and this went on for four weeks during the winter. I could see the other kids were playing in the snow and I was missing out. So I told my mother I was sick of going and she said I could stop. When the woman came to see where I was, my mother told her I was ill. Later on I was going out the front door and the woman collared me for not going for her messages. She said, 'Its all right for your mother, she is young enough to do her own.' When my mother heard what she had said she blew her top and told me I was never to go for this woman's messages again.

Joyce Carlson

Runny Butter

There was no such thing as a fridge. When you bought butter at some shops it was often all runny and there were flies around it.

Olga Carlson

Scarlet Fever

In 1935 I fell ill with scarlet fever and I had to go into the Deans Isolation Hospital. They used to call it the fever hospital in those days. The ambulance came to our house in South Frederick Street and I was wrapped in a large red wool blanket and carried inside. Then the fumigation people came and fumigated the room. The smell was still there four weeks later when I came out of hospital. For the first week in the Deans I was so ill I couldn't eat, then on the second week I could eat some soup. By the third week we were being served mince and potatoes. That was the first time I ate meat because when I was young I didn't like the idea of eating a dead animal. Every evening the nurse used to come around the ward and put a towel on our shoulders and comb us for head lice. Everyone in the ward had head lice. Shortly after I returned, my brother was taken ill with scarlet fever and then my mother was taken in as well and she was really bad. She had to have a tracheotomy. When she came out she had arthritis and she couldn't walk for a year afterwards.

Joyce Carlson

I had Scarlet Fever when I was about five or six. My bed was taken downstairs to the front room. Then the room was completely sealed and fumigated. I couldn't leave the room, which was in darkness, because all of the windows and door were sealed. My mother had worked at the Whiteleas Infectious Diseases Hospital so she had some experience to cope with me.

Ken Corner

My Treat

My eldest brother was a fireman on the railway line up to Consett. He would take tea to work in a lemonade bottle and it used to stand on the hotplate in the cab all day. My treat was getting what was left in the bottle at the end of the day. I used to loved the taste.

Dave Ditchburn

Ha'penny Duck

On the way to the Palace Picture House in South Frederick Street for the Saturday afternoon matinee we used to call in at Fishers the pork butchers and get a Ha'penny Duck. It was a sort of meatball and that fed us in the pictures.

Tom Dawson

In The Back Garden

Where the houses on Mitford Road are now, behind Temple Park Road, was all fields when I was young. There was a dyke in the middle with brambles which used to separate the land into two fields. Nora Strang and Nat Strang, who was a bigwig over at Harton Hospital, used to keep horses in the field for children with polio to ride. I would give them a hand to lead the horses around the field. Then the field was bought by builders, the houses

Deans Isolation Hospital, Dean Road, 1912. (Courtesy South Tyneside Libraries.)

24

Horses on the field between Temple Park Road and King George Road.

started going up and the horses went over to Whiteleas.

Raymond Wilkinson

Part Time Money

My brother Albert Wilkinson used to make toffee cakes in the wash-house and sell them on the back step. When someone wanted to buy one he would carry the tray downstairs. If they picked one with a cross they got another toffee cake free. With the money he bought a bike and a tent.

Joyce Carlson

Chickens In An Alcove

People had no awareness of hygiene. Neighbours of ours used to keep chickens in an alcove in the kitchen. In another family, a child was scalded with hot fat and none of them ever thought about taking her to the hospital. The dad put her on the table and burst her blisters with a needle. She was screaming with the pain. People put butter on burns instead of cold water and sent their children out to play in the street with big wedges of bread, margarine and jam when their hands were scruffy.

Mary Peterson

Gas Filled Balloons

My father bought me a long gas filled balloon from Woolworth's. I was playing with it in the kitchen and it went up the chimney. The fire was on at the time, and my mother had a bowl of flower and lard on the fender. It was tipped up so the fire would melt the lard. My father said to me, 'Have you got any darts?' They were wooden darts with wooden points and we went up on to the kitchen roof and managed to burst the balloon by throwing darts down the chimney. But when it burst a shower of soot came down the chimney and filled up the bowl. My mother gave us both hell about that.

Ernie Keedy

Snadgy Wagon.

During the war the fields around the cliff tops were all cultivated and me and my mates used to fill the bogie with turnips and bring them back home for dinner. We called it the Snadgy Wagon.

Tom Dawson

We used to camp out on Camels Island with a clothes horse and a blanket. On the way down we would pinch taties and turnips from the fields to eat during the night

Ernie Keedy

I Had To Walk

When I was eleven my parents couldn't afford my fair from the Law Top to Westoe Secondary School. Even if they could, I would still have had to walk as far as Moon Street for

the tram and then get off at Mowbray Road and walk up. So I had to walk to school everyday via the bridge at Erskine Road.

Isabella Meyers

Bath Night

A bath was never a private event. I can remember being chased up the back lane by my mother to get me in the zinc bath in front of the fire and the family. We never went short, but settees always had springs sticking out, carpets never quite met the wall and colours were never co-ordinated. But because of that I think houses had a lively feel

Ken Carter

New Batteries

When we lived in South Frederick Street we had a big radio set and about once a year my brother Albert and I went to a house in Eldon Street on a Sunday to get a new battery for it. The man always seemed to be getting his Sunday dinner whenever we called and always wore a white shirt and a waistcoat with a gold watch. The battery was a big container with a purple fluid inside that might have been acid because we had to carry the container very carefully back home.

Joyce Carlson

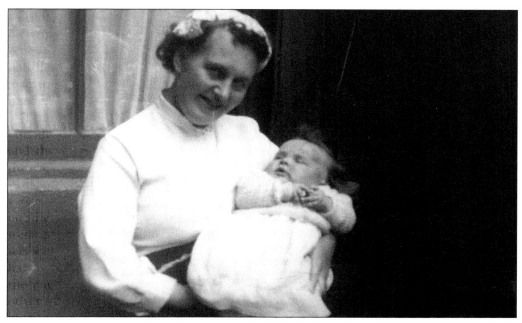

Ken Carter with his mother.

Almost Like Sunderland

We used to get the tram from Tyne Dock to Westoe and then get off by the fountain. From there we would get another tram up King George Road to the Ridgeway and walk up to Cleadon hills. To us children from around Tyne Dock, being at Cleadon was almost like being in Sunderland.

Tom Dawson

Hot Broken Wafers And

Lemonade

I used to come out of Derby Street Baths absolutely starving and go to Gabrielle's to get a pennies worth of hot broken wafers. I can still taste the flavour, it sticks in the memory like the taste of a Dickson's pork sandwich.

After the wafers, we bought lemonade from an old woman who made her own but wouldn't let you take the bottle away. You had to drink it on the spot and give her the bottle straight back and she refilled it for the next person.

Michael Minchella

You held your jumper out and a chap used to come along with a shovel and fill it with the wafers that had dropped on to the floor and fallen in all sorts of places.

Tom Dawson

Bontie Nights

On 'bontie nights', before there were laws to stop people doing daft things to themselves, we would build massive bonfires at the back of South

Frederick Street where the old miners' cottages used to be. We would go bontie collecting, knocking on people's doors and asking if they had, 'anything for the bontie', and we would be given things like old wardrobes and three piece suites. We would go through them looking for money and find all sorts of threepenny bits, tanners, old florins, two bob bits and sometimes a dollar (five shilling). Then we also used to go bontie raiding to pinch wood from other peoples bonties and if we were really brave we would go to the Deans Estate where all the hard lads used to live. When the Deans came to raid our bontie we would have to retreat. To retaliate we would make banger bombs out of the gunpowder from fireworks, an old bit of pipe and a big ball baring. We would set it off and, bang! The ball bearing would go flying and luckily the accuracy was crap and we never hit anyone.

Sometimes someone would set your bontie alight a few days before bonfire night and you would have to scour the streets for old doors and sideboards so you would have something to burn for bontie night. Each year the piles of wood got bigger and so of course did the flames. Once our bontie was so big the fire brigade had to come and hose down people's doors because the paint was cracking and they were worried they were going to burst into flames. Often the fire would still be burning the next day and we would rake through it looking for old springs and the fused bits of bottles we had thrown in. We would stink of smoke and ash for days afterwards.

John Weir

Pay Day

Friday was always quite an event for us because my dad worked at Wardly Pit and that was when he came home with his pay packet. With my pocket money I went down the lane to Greenwood's on the corner of Westoe Road. The shop had a low curved window and around the bottom was a display of matchbox cars on top of their boxes and that was what I spent my money on.

Ken Carter

Beside The Railway Line

At Biddick Hall estate was a group of houses beside the railway line that ran up to Consett. On summer days, the housewives would have their washing out on the line, happily drying away. Then there would be a rumble in the ground. Through my feet I could almost perceive a great weight coming towards me. There would be a loud roar and a belching noise, the back doors would fly open and the women would start shouting to each other and grab the still damp washing off the line. Then a great big dirty black steam engine, throwing out a load of black smoke and clag, would move past the houses. The smoke would drift over the back gardens and if the washing was out, it would ruin it. When I first saw this it looked highly hilarious and I think that's why I started to like steam engines and still like them to this day.

Eddie Post

CHAPTER 2
Schooldays

The Boys High School Gym Display Team. The gym teacher, Mr Gray, is on the left. Bill Henderson jnr is on the top of the pyramid. This position was called the 'sack' because on command all of the boys would throw their arms forwards and the pyramid would collapse.

On The First Day

I was first taught in an old wooden hut on Prince Edward Road, just before you came to the New Crown. You had to go up three or four steps then you were in the classroom. When I was seven I went into the main school next door in East Avenue.

Bill Salkeld

The first day I had to go to school was dreadful. I had never been away from my mother, but she was looking forward to getting me to school. She talked about it all the time. On the first day this very nice teacher, Miss Davidson, who was very motherly, said to me, 'Hello, come along, sit in a desk.' To which I replied, 'I'm not going to sit in a desk!' She said, 'Oh but you must.' But I was firm, 'I'm not going to sit in a desk, and I'm not going to sit beside her!' I pointed at the little girl I was supposed to sit beside. I don't know why, I just did. However, my mother forced me into the desk and said, 'Stay there, you must. Everybody else is staying here.' Then she was told by the teacher to go away from the classroom. However, I had other ideas and I stood on the top of the desk. I could just see over the top of the door when I was on tiptoe and I knew my mother was outside. I repeated over and over again, 'Mammy talk to me teacher, mammy talk to me teacher.' I don't know why. I think the teacher was a little bit upset. However, they had in the classroom a big rocking horse designed to take four children. I liked that and for the first three months at school all my lessons were taken sitting on the rocking horse because I wouldn't sit at a desk. In 1927 I was taught by Miss Grimes. She was very fond of reading us stories and I would sit fascinated on a Friday as she read about Peter Pan, and Cinderella. She read with such expression. Then she decided she was going to get the class to act them out so I put my hand up because I thought these stories were lovely and I wanted to be picked. But she said, 'You can't be in the front line looking like that. You've got hair like a lion's main.' I was most put out about that but I still liked her stories. Towards the end of her career she got the little girls to line up and pretend to be various kinds of flowers and asked them to sway in the wind. Then she went around and watered them all with a real watering can. Of course the parents objected when the girls went home soaking wet.

Isabella Meyers

I used to be quite nervous as a child but the first day I went to school, Miss Collie, my first teacher, took us all by the hand and danced us down the corridor to the classroom. I can remember my mother looking in through the classroom window as I happily played away with Plastercine. I loved it and never had any problems about school.

Kathleen Burdon

Greenfingers

I went to Mowbray Road Infants School and that was where I first got interested in gardening. We used to have little bits of soil to grow things in.

Barnes Road School in the 1980s.(Courtesy The Shields Gazette)

Ernie Keedy

Nuns Knocking At The Front Door

My mother had been a Catholic and we all went to the Victoria Road Catholic School. After she died, my father tried to take us out and that caused a huge hubbub. The priest came to the house, the nuns from the convent at Westoe village came to the house and they all tried to get me to stay because it was unheard of for anyone to leave a Catholic school. The nuns also wanted me to go into the convent, but I wasn't having that because I never got on very well with them. They came around on a Friday, when we weren't supposed to eat meat, but we had mince and dumplings on Fridays so as soon as we heard the nuns knocking at the front door we used hide the dinner in the back bedroom. I think the nuns knew what we had been doing because mince smells nothing like fish.

Olga Carlson

Coincidence

I went to St Aidan's prep school at Sunderland and you would have thought I would have been the envy of the other children as I had a father who ran an ice cream shop. Well there were five other children in my class whose fathers were in the ice cream business which I found to be a very strange coincidence. However, the school never had any trouble getting ice cream for sports day.

Michael Minchella

Notes For Medication

A nurse used to come around to check for nits and after the examination we used to try to find out who had the notes for medication. Everyone used to try to hide the slips of paper from each other.

Mary Peterson

Terribly Strict

We had a woman teacher who was built like a man with really broad shoulders and she was terribly strict. She just used to look at you and you would curl up. She had a fierce face and that was enough to terrify anyone. One day someone had done something when she was writing on the board. I can't remember what it was but she turned around and said, 'Come out! Whoever did that come out to the front.' We knew who had done it but the girl in question was too frightened to go out and we wouldn't spill the beans. So the teacher said 'Will somebody tell me who it was?' Nobody would split on her. By this time she was getting really annoyed so she said, 'Right that's it you'll all get punished.' She got this big cane with a frayed end out of the cupboard. We all had to line up around her desk and in turn we held out our hands and got the cane. She really hurt us hard. She was vicious and had a cruel streak in her. However, there were about forty of us in the class and she put that much energy into it that she fainted and fell flat out on the floor. One of us had to go and get the headmistress who came running in and there was such a fuss. When we got outside we were all laughing and thought serve her right. It was great.

Jean Cockayne

Mr Two Dinners

One of the teachers at Ocean Road School was a bully. When we were having school dinners he sat at the head of our table and he used to demand two dinners from the kitchen staff and he always got them. When the old bottle of sauce was finished everyone took their turn to buy a new bottle. The turn would go around the table, Joe, then Billy, then Peter. Now every time a new bottle was bought for our table he used half of it on his dinners, the rest would be left to divide between fifteen or twenty boys and the last would often get nothing. I still meet people from school and he's one of the teachers they all remember.

Alfred Beris

Taking The Teacher Home

One Christmas I was given a large wooden dolls house. The front opened up and it was full of furniture and there were even electric lights inside operated by a battery. I was thrilled to bits with this. When we went back to school in Barnes Road and the teacher Miss Jessop asked what we had got for Christmas I told her all about it and then asked if she would like come around and see it. She said yes and I kept her to her word because I can remember nagging at her to come around to see the dolls house. Eventually she and another teacher came with me to my home in 192, South Frederick Street. When my mother opened the front door and saw the two teachers standing there she thought I had been in trouble. But I explained and invited them in. It was good of them to come around but later I realised that they must have thought it was a huge joke.

Joyce Carlson

Growing Up

St John's was a good school, and you could tell that because most of the people who later went to work at the Town Hall went there. The thing I really remember about starting there was the sudden transformation that came over me because for the first time there were girls in the class. They were fourteen and fifteen and starting to mature. I became aware of how I looked and how I dressed. I wanted to wear a tie instead of a gansey jumper and I started to wash my face and comb my hair. At dinner time some of them had earrings in and the teachers used to tell them to take their earrings out and make-up off.

Ernie Keedy

Joyce Carlson (nee Wilkinson) outside her home at No. 192, South Frederick street in 1934.

English The Hard Way

When I was young I didn't like anyone touching my turban because my religion is very important to me. At school there was a lad called Ted and he used to touch my turban so we always used to fight a lot. I couldn't speak a lot of English because we had been moving around, so I got into a lot of trouble because I couldn't explain to the teacher what was going on and why I was always getting into fights. Ted is a friend of mine now and he ended up doing me a favour because it made me learn English very fast and the hard way.

Pupils of the Catholic School, Derby Terrace, 1936. Olga Carlson (nee Hargemann) is first left in the middle row.

A class from St John's School, 1931. Evelyn Drew (nee Lawrenson) is in the back row, extreme left. Below Evelyn is Doris McGurk and below her is Bob Hedley.

The wedding of M.S. Shabilla's youngest son, Sukdave Singh, 22 June 1986.

When I was fourteen, Ted was the captain of the school football team and he always picked me to be on his side. We both had a trial for Newcastle at St James' Park, but because my father used to think there would be no money in football, I didn't get the boots I needed. So I couldn't go to the trial. I cried and cried about it, but that was that.

M.S. Shabilla

A Gold Star

The Catholic school was down Victoria Road next to St Bede's church. The first thing the teachers asked on the morning was who had gone to communion and you got a gold star if you had gone. People weren't supposed to have anything to eat before communion, but my dad would never let us go out the house until we had a breakfast, so I never had any gold stars. One day I was so desperate for a star, because I had had a telling off at school, I did go to communion anyway. When I came out of the church, my brothers and sisters were all convinced I would be struck dead. On the Friday we had to hold hands and walk into the church to go to confession. I was only six or seven and in a small child's eyes you never think you have done anything wrong. We used to stay up at night worrying about what we were going to say and that was the most terrifying experience in my life. We took confession in a very overpowering black confession box. There seemed to be nothing there. You just heard a voice coming through the mesh.

Olga Carlson

For some reason the playground at the Catholic school was built on the roof. Walking past, I was always amazed to see this.

Harry Peasland

Cleadon Park

I thought Cleadon Park was a fantastic school. We had 'Domestic', as we called it, in a room with a beautiful bathroom, bedroom and kitchen. I couldn't understand why no one lived in it.

Olga Carlson

A Little Bit Rough

I had started secondary school at Dean Road but after a few months I went up to Cleadon Park. They were much more open minded at Cleadon Park. On my first test I got the best score in my class and I don't think the teachers liked that because it made their standards look second best. There was a PE teacher there who was, in my opinion, a little bit rough with the lads. We had to climb the ropes to the ceiling then drop down. A lad we called Fatty Arbuckle could only go up a few feet and this teacher would grasp the end of the rope and whack him across the backside with it to make him climb further. I think the teacher later left the school after an incident with a vaulting horse and a broken arm.

Hugh Amess

A lot of us had been involved in a fight at Cleadon Park School and when we were caught, this Scotch maths teacher gave us the choice of detention, lines or the stick. The rest were either choosing detention or lines but I couldn't be bothered so I asked for the stick. The teacher then let me go and gave everyone else the stick.

Harry Peasland

High School

With the school scholarship, or eleven plus as it became, there wasn't a pass mark. It was a question of how many places were available at the Boys High School and at the Girls High School. They would take as many children as they could, then the rest went to secondary moderns. My marks were good enough to get me to the Girls High School and I was amazed at just being there. The school made us all feel special. We wore a uniform and in those days nobody else wore one. For the girls it was fawn lisle stockings, brown lace-up shoes, a white square neck long sleeve blouse and a navy blue gym slip, like a smock. The material hung in three box pleats at the front and three at the back and that didn't flatter anyone, no matter what your figure was. They were horrible when I think about them. You also wore a girdle around your waist either blue, red, green or yellow depending on what house you were in. If you were on one of the school teams then you wore a very special one, dark blue, light blue and yellow. We had to wear a felt hat with a brim and the school badge at the front. During the war the older girls wore their hair in the fashionable styles, usually swept up very high at the front and long at the back. These pork pie hats wouldn't fit on the hair so we would pleat them around the crown and fix them to our hair with hat pins. If you were seen like that you were straight in the head's room for a very good talking too.

Ethel Dawson

Grey Socks With Yellow Stripes

At the age of eleven I got through the eleven plus and went to the Grammar School at Harton. I got the No. 11 bus from Laygate up to the Nook with my friend Ken. We were scared witless because we both had these brand new uniforms on and we really stood out. We had short trousers, grey socks with yellow stripes across the top and a cap that you had to wear. If you were seen in school without the cap on you could be punished. Sometimes teachers would even stop their cars in St Mary's Avenue and tell you to put your cap on. We walked into the school yard terrified. The school was on a far larger scale than what we had been used to at Laygate. We were going from a hall that held about three hundred pupils, to one that held over a thousand. But we soon met this lad called Brian who was in second year. He knew us from Laygate and knew what it would be like for us and he looked after us.

Malcolm Grady

'Pan', 'Spuggy', Charlie and 'Piggy'

I can still remember the good teachers at the Boys Grammar School. There was 'Pan' Headly, 'Spuggy' Wesencraft, Charlie Constable and 'Piggy' Wade who taught history. There was only one teacher who we were scared of, Mr 'Mif' Moffet. He was a little round fellow who could terrify the whole class just by looking at them. The only problem was that teachers would come and go because of the war and that caused many of us problems with lessons.

Ken Corner

Writing On The Board

Mr Micham, my teacher in fourth year juniors, introduced us to a very wide range of ideas. We listened to *Peer Gynt* live on the radio and we had to imagine the story from the music. It was in his class that I was allowed to write on the blackboard for the first time. That was something only the teachers were allowed to do and it was a fantastic boost to your confidence being able to stand at the front of the class and do something like that.

Malcolm Grady

Football Strip

The school football strip was immaculate. It was Cambridge and Oxford quarters with a yellow collar, yellow trim on the sleeve, white shorts and the two blues and a yellow hooped socks. It was so distinctive. We used to travel all over with the team. We went to Morpeth, Sunderland, Newcastle and the north side of the Tyne. When we played at Boldon Colliery we used to get changed in the Co-op undertakers

Malcom Grady.

amongst the coffins before we walked across the road to the field. The lads used to say, 'Our match is a dead cert.'

Tom Dawson

Having The Teacher On

At the Boys High School, every time we changed subject, we changed classrooms. The door into the class was partitioned off by a wooded blast proof screen and the idea was that when the bell went, those pupils leaving would go around one side while those coming in would enter from the other. If we were having the teacher on we would just go out around one side then straight back in around the other and there was a continuous of stream of boys coming into the class. Some of the teachers couldn't understand what was happening and we had a good laugh, but we couldn't get away with that with all of them.

Tom Dawson

The Haircut

The headmaster of the Boys Grammar School, Mr Egner, was very much ahead of his time. He brought in a lecturer from Durham University to teach Chinese history, installed the first computer into a school in the country and he was the first to introduce statistics as a separate subject. One day he collared me and said, 'Grady, come and see me at two o'clock.' When you went in to see him you waited in the secretary's room until the light went on and then you knew you could go in. When I went in he said to me, 'Grady, I'm going to give it to you straight. You're letting the school down, your hair is too long. I want you to get it cut and I am going to give you half a crown. Go directly to the hairdressers, get you hair cut and come back and see me.' I could not believe this. I took the half a crown and went out of his room. But I didn't get my hair cut because it was Friday night and club night and if I had got my hair cut my social life would have been gone. On the Monday I was called to account. I went along to see him, gave him his money back and told him I couldn't do it. He put me on detention. I can't remember exactly how this was resolved but I think we compromised with a slight trim.

Malcolm Grady

Fancy A Fight?

If you wanted to have a fight with someone at school you would goad them. But there was a certain code that had to be followed when the blows started. Although we used to brag a lot about who could fight who, there was no going for someone when their back was turned, no kicking and if you hit someone when they were down on the ground the other lads would call you a coward.

Hugh Amess

The Builders Lime Pits

I would walk to school with Colin Green who lived in Ashley Road. His father was the butcher in Boldon Lane. On the way home at dinner time, we decided to play on the building site between Ashley Road and Talbot Road. In those days the builders had lime pits to slake the lime for the plaster. There was this big square lime pond and we started to play around it. After a while we were getting plaster all over us and forgetting that it was dinner time. My father came out looking for me and found us both. By this time we should really have been back at school and we got into a hell of a lot of trouble because we were covered in plaster and we had to be thoroughly scrubbed down before we could go back.

Ken Corner

Pellets Of Iron Ore

Me and my friends used to get on our bikes, peddle down to Tyne Dock and try to dodge the security men at the council depot. Once across the depot we would fill our pockets with iron ore that had dropped out of the trucks that ran up the line to Consett Steelworks. It was the perfect catapult ammunition, just like little musket balls. Then we would sneak back over the estate and peddle back home. We had the best catapult ammunition a schoolboy could want. It was brilliant, but deadly.

Eddie Post

Terrified

I didn't really enjoy my school days because I was always terrified of the teachers. They used to rattle me. You got the cane for anything. If you were a minute late you got the cane.

Mary Peterson

St Hilda's Youth Club

In the early 1960s St Hilda's youth club had the best reputation in the town for live music and you were really proud that you had one of their membership cards. This was the time of Mods and Rockers and there used to be Lambrettas lined up outside the club. It was quite a place to be.

Malcolm Grady

Alfred Beris, aged 11.

Cleadon Park School Netball Team, 1953. The PE Teacher is Miss Bell and the headmistress is Miss Atchinson. The girls include: Maureen Heslop, Jean Slater, Eva Meeks, Margaret Meeks and Ann Smith

Pupils of Harton Juniors, 1949. Jean Slater is front left.

CHAPTER 3
Working Life

The tug *Langton* attends a cargo ship in the Tyne in 1948. (Courtesy Beamish Museum)

Jane Scott, mother of Jean Shanahan, at Marsden Beach around 1920.

Either A Saver Or A Spender

If you were a wife of a seafarer you were either a saver or a spender, there was no middle way. Fortunately for us when the slump came in the 1920s, my mother had been a saver. Not everyone was as lucky. One of my relatives married a sea captain, a master mariner. He was considered quite a good catch but unfortunately she lost her head with pride. He was laid up for three years and they were very short of money which was quite traumatic because she had been one of Grant's the jewellers favourite customers. My mother's mother-in-law was always a profligate spender and she veered from living in the lap of luxury to having to move house because of a change in her financial circumstances. When her husband, who was also a master mariner, came home the butter disappeared out of the butter dish and was replaced by margarine to show him how hard up they all were. During the slump the master mariners were working in the Marine Park gardens because they hadn't any other work. My mother used to say that sea captains were now ten a penny in Woolworth's, but you could go to the Marine Park and pick one up for nothing.

Jean Shanahan

The Demands Of Work

My first job was at a firm of plumbers and the man in charge was very strange. In the office you had to keep all the bits of paper turned face down in case anyone came in and saw his business. He was always washing his hands, always dressed immaculately and always had rings on. He had eyes like a hawk and he used to give the plumbers hell. They all used to hate him. His wife was a proper lady, all fur coats and things. She couldn't bear to come into the office and smell the tin baths. They used to have the apprentices go up to their house to beat the carpets because she wasn't well. After leaving the plumbers I did a secretarial course at the technical college and after that I started at a chemist beside the Market Square as a shorthand typist. The boss had his own office and when you went in to see him it was like going in to see God. The girl in charge of the switchboard was called Norma and even though she was

Bill Corner (extreme left) with pit ponies near Westoe Village during the 1926 Miners' Strike.

just my age she was always very fashionably dressed and always looked very impressive. When one of the girls was getting married they said they would all be going to the wedding and I would have to man the switchboard. I didn't know how it worked. To me it was all plugs and cables, like one of those you see in old films. After an hour of things getting worse and worse I just burst into tears and pulled all the plugs out. On Monday morning the rest of the staff got slaughtered by the boss for leaving me there untrained and on my own. I wasn't with the company for much longer after that. On the dinner time I went to a furnishing shop and got a new job. It was great there, just like a holiday camp. I was working for an accounts inspector and he was supposed to keep an eye open for non payers and fiddles. The company had a lot of accounts that were behind and he used to stand in the office saying, 'Tell the buggers if they don't pay up, they are going to court, that'll frighten the buggers.' Then later the company found out why so many accounts were behind. He was fiddling the books himself. He was fiddling everyone.

Mary Peterson

A Churn Of Blood

I had a job as a butcher's boy for Harry Smith who had a shop at Horsley Hill Square. One of my jobs was to pedal the delivery bike with a big milk churn in the basket to the slaughterhouse and fill it up with blood for the black puddings. One day as I was pedalling back I skidded, the churn came out of the basket and the blood spilt right across the road. I had to go back and get

43

another one. I think Harry stopped the money for it out of my wages.

Hugh Amess

Down The Mine

I had four brothers and they all went to work down the mine. My father didn't want them to, but going down the mine was the big thing at the time so that's what they did. My father was a 'hewer'. He did about forty years at Whitburn alone and he had the usual symptoms, the coughing and the lung problems. There were no conveyer belts in the pits in the 1920s. The coal had to be filled into tubs and it had to be putted out, drawn out with a pony in a set. The man that brought it out was called a putter, he used to get about 9d a tub. If you had a 'canny cabal' it meant that you had a good pitch in the mine. If you are cutting coal with a pick, and it's a

good seam, then you would get a lot out. My brother Tom had a better spot than most people and being a single lad he used to be able to provide our mother with quite a bit of money.

Bob Hedley

Sacked?

My brother Albert Wilkinson wanted to be a joiner but the depression was on and it was a bad year to begin to serve your time. For a while he worked for the Newcastle Tea Company in Westoe Road, taking orders out on a bike. When he was fifteen, the manager, Mr Manors, wanted to put him behind the counter but Albert said that he didn't want to work with a lot of women. One day he came home and said he had been sacked. Our mother was very surprised. The next day he went down to the Mill Dam labour pool

St Hilda's Colliery, c. 1930. Isaac Wilkinson is third left in the front row.

44

Hugh Amess driving the company van outside the West End Garage in 1956.

where the merchant navy men got jobs. He signed up as a cabin boy and went off to sea. Three days later our mother was walking past the shop and Mr Manors was standing outside and he asked her if she could not persuade Albert to come back. He could not understand why Albert had been so keen to leave.

Joyce Carlson

The West End Garage

I served my time at the West End Garage. It was good fun but conditions were pretty bad. It was like an old shack with a corrugated roof and in the winter it was freezing. One day an ice cream van came in for a service. I put it on the inspection lift and pressed the button, but I forgot how tall ice cream vans are and smashed part of its roof in. I also filled up the cars at the pumps. A well respected South Shields doctor came in one day driving a long sports car. He asked me to blow up the tyres, which I did, then he asked me to blow up the spare in the boot. I opened the boot and it was full of bricks. He told me the tyre was underneath them. I asked him why the bricks were there and he said they were to ballast the car as it swung around corners. In those days tyres were often used past the point when they were completely bald and I think he thought the bricks would give him a bit more stability. If tyres got a split in them all the drivers would do was take the tyre off and put what they called a vulcanised garter on. That blended into the tyre, then they would just blow it up and drive off.

Hugh Amess

45

Wright's Biscuits card: 'Mischief Goes to Mars'.

Wright's Biscuits

I was a delivery driver for Wright's biscuits. I loaded up the van with the big tins then drove off to places like Great Yarmouth. We packed the van with the first delivery at the back because the tins were individually packaged up for each shop and you wouldn't be able to get them out otherwise. I would be away for three days at a time and at night I used to sleep in the van. The smell of the broken biscuits from the factory was amazing. They used to have a kid with ginger hair on the packets and we would call him Gingernuts.

Hugh Amess

A Job During Wartime

In my final year at school I went to Hawthorn Leslie's to sit a test for shipyard draftsmen. I failed. I spoke to my teacher Mr Gill who suggested I become an architect. I contacted Mr Page of the company Page and Bradbury at 75, King Street who took me on for ten bob a week because almost all of his staff had been called up for the Second World War. He was a First World War man and a gentleman in the old fashioned sense. There wasn't a lot of building work going on because of the war, but we did have to measure up bomb damaged buildings. Every day we would be walking through dirty water and slimy rubble. Going into damaged buildings gave you a real insight into how other people lived and worked. To say some of the buildings were primitive is not an adequate description, they were often filthy. We would all have to clamber over the mess, measuring up with a tape measure, except for old Mr Farthing who was well over seventy-years-old. Mr Farthing had the most amazing skill. He could just look at the room and tell you what its dimensions were within an inch. The boss, Mr Page, had a daughter who was a little bit younger than me. They lived in Grovener Road and had a tennis court. On some afternoons, when there was nothing for me to do at work, he would tell me to go up there and teach his daughter to play tennis.

Ken Corner

The Energy To Smile

I worked at Harton Colliery as a timekeeper, timing the men going down and timing when they came back up. There were three shifts running constantly and I had to keep track of who was down and who was up. When they were getting ready to go on shift the men would all congregate together in a waiting area beside the pit shaft swapping stories and jokes. I would see them about eight hours later and they were completely black with the coal dust. It was amazing though how many of them still had the energy to smile when they came back out.

John Inskip

Harton's Electrics

On the 25 July 1952 I started work as an electrical engineer with the National Coal Board. My first job was to help put the lighting in the low staiths tunnel under Commercial Road. We were lying on our backs on a raised platform, hand drilling holes in the ceiling … bash … bash … bash … then we clipped the wires for the lights in. I came out black as a crow. At that time it could only take the old ten ton wooden coal wagons and the Coal Board wanted to bring in the twenty ton hoppers. The tunnel was widened in

stages during the night so they didn't have to stop the flow of wagons. Each night a few yards of the old brickwork was knocked out, two pre-cast sections slid in, then the overhead wire re-installed for the next day. Then the next night the same thing again. There were no lights outside of the workshops and if you were working in the sidings it was a torch job. Then when I was eighteen they started putting light all the way through.

Coal from Harton, Whitburn and Boldon came down to the old dry cleaner at Westoe where it was segregated by compressed air and vibrators. The cleaner was six floors tall, about ninety feet high. The coal was teamed on to a conveyer, then run up to the top. The first thing that happened was it was run over a guide tray with a magnet above it to take the metal out. Then the coal dropped down to the next floor where it was segregated into the big and small chunks, then on the floor below the heavier stone was shaken out. By the end of the process the coal was running as smooth as water. It was beautiful. Then it dropped down through the loader into the wagons. I remember one of the men who worked there was called Jimmy Gilpin. The wagons never stopped moving through that loader and when they came out, they had four little humps of coal on top so identical you would think they had measured them with a rule. There was only about six electricians who looked after everything – the dry cleaner, the shipping staiths, Marsden Quarry, the railway's overhead wiring and the locomotives – everything electrical that wasn't actually inside a pit.

Bill Henderson Jnr fixing over head wire on the High Staiths track. High Shields station is behind.

Nothing had to stop the pit or the flow of coal. That was the top priority because coal was our bread and butter and the town gasworks still had to be fed with coal on Christmas Day, New Years Day, everyday. If a breakdown occurred, you had to go out and fix it even if you had just clocked off shift. Quite often the electric locos would come off the track and sometimes all the overhead would be down and we would have to run around the houses getting people in. We had to physically jack the locos up and then push them back on to the track. That was hell of a job. When we let them go fifty tons of metal would come clashing down on to the rails and you had to judge it right or the flanges would fall on the other side of the rails and you would have to start again. At the same time as this was going on we would have people digging holes to put new overhead poles in and others trying to mend the tracks. We

did have some big accidents. Someone went through a red light at Victoria Road, buried the loco in the bankside and blocked the track with the wagons. That meant Harton Colliery was cut off and we had to work all day and all night getting it out with only the occasional climb over the wall to the Cyprus for a couple of pints.

If you looked at St Hilda Colliery you would just see the shaft, some buildings and a load of railway lines, but underneath there was stables and all sorts. I got lost down there once. That whole area was honeycombed. There was even a tunnel that ran underneath station bank right through to Commercial Road. The trip through the tunnel to the low staiths was an experience because the gradient at the staiths end was so steep the trains couldn't stop. After they had gained a bit of practice at it the drivers would let their trains hurtle down that bend

The NCB locomotive shed at Westoe Colliery around 1983. Locomotive No. 4 (right) dates from 1909.
A hydraulic jack for lifting de-railed locomotives is standing at the back of the shed.

because at the other end of the tunnel there was a very steep curve that slowed the trains right down again. It was frightening if you didn't know what was going on because as well as the feeling of speed, the noise and the darkness, the curve was so tight the wagon handbreaks would be screeching against the tunnel wall. Once they were at the staiths the wagons were shunted into the unloading lines by force of gravity. The tracks were laid out so there was always a declining gradient in the right direction until they were finally collected by another electric engine and pulled back to the pit.

The railway began closing with the pits, until all that was left was the system for Westoe Colliery. Then only a few years before they shut the pit they decided to concentrate coal shipping at the new terminal at Tyne Dock. They allowed British Rail to take over the route to Tyne Dock and the line down Erskine Bank was replaced with a conveyer belt to get the slurry down to Harton Low Staiths. That was the end of the electric railway. I think it was a purely political decision to close Harton Staiths because we could load faster than Tyne Dock and although they said they could load bigger ships than us, we were loading twelve thousand toners at the finish.

Bill Henderson Jnr

The last shale wagon to be teamed at Harton Staiths stands in Hilda Sidings on Wednesday 19 July 1989. In front are driver Jim Holman, fifth from left, and guard John Stewart, fourth from left. Behind is the St Hilda Winding Shaft. (Photo Bill Hatcher, author The Harton Electric Railway)

Jean Cockayne.

The Pilots' Office

When I worked at the Shields pilots' office beside the river, Sid Johnson was the pilot master and used to live in a big flat above the offices. I would help sort out the wages and the schedules and handle any complaints. The pilots were always paid for the amount of hours they worked and that had to be sorted out at the end of the week. We sat facing the harbour and we had a wonderful view. Once I asked Mr Kennedy, who ran the office, if we could have a rise in our pay. He said, 'Ask for a rise with a beautiful view like that you should be paying me!' He was still a nice man to work for though. In the 1960s the river was heaving. I would say that there were about eighty pilots and they were working all the time. The river was thriving. There would be ships kept waiting outside of the piers. Stevenson Clark used to own most of the colliers. Then they all faded away. We didn't take any more pilots on as the old ones retired. They closed the office down in the 1980s. Now you're lucky if you see one ship in the distance.

Jean Cockayne

On The Tugs

The best job I had was on the tugs. When I started there were about twenty-eight of them on the Tyne and I used to work the ropes. In the summer the fruit boats came in from Australia and from around the world. We took *The City of Durban* up the Tyne to discharge the tinned fruit at Newcastle and the dockers used to give us the dented tins. We would bust them open and drink the juice.

If there were ships due, then you had to work. It was well-paid work, but you had to put the hours in for it. I was never at home. Riddley's got the orders in about what ships were due for the Tyne from the various shipping companies. The tug would lie out at the buoys and we used to skull across to the quay and get the list for the day. An hour before the ship was due we used to be inside the piers so when the ship crossed the bar we would be ready to let the line go. If a ship had to go up to Mercantile dry dock we used to have to swing her around. If she was a canny length we would do it at Jarrow Staiths, the widest part of the river. It would take four tugs, one forward and one aft, then two to bridle her. Then we swung her straight around. If it was too rough for the ships to come into the Tyne, they would lie off the coast, well outside the piers. A Greek boat once went aground on The Groyne. The tugs had let her go too soon. We tried to salvage her and we would have got a share of

River Tyne tugs escort an aircraft carrier which contains a touring Festival of Britain exhibition.

Brighams yard, 1961.

the salvage money. We had a hellish long tow rope on her because we had to watch for ourselves for the tide, but the boat was too fast aground, nearly up on to the road. In the end they just broke her up where she was. Burnt her up and took it all away.

We used to go to North Shields every morning to pick the firemen up from the quayside and one of them used to come down each day with his wife. As we went across we would see them standing kissing each other. Then as the tug got over they would kiss each other ta ra and he would turn to walk off down the ladder. Then he would change his mind and go back to her again. The skipper used to say, 'This is breaking my heart.' As we were going across the lads used to sing, 'We are sailing.'

If you're working on ocean going tugs you had to go out in heavy seas – force nine and ten. Sometimes you couldn't get alongside to get the rope on. On our tug you didn't have the gun to fire the hawser. We weren't equipped for deep sea work. When we were towing *The Leader* with the new diesel tugs the *Impetus* and *Maximus*, the skipper did not know how much weight to put on the hawser. Well, it snapped, and killed the lad on deck. He was only eighteen.

One time we had to go to Flambera Head. There was a collier sheltering there. The gale was bad and the skipper was shouting for assistance. When we were bringing her in, I was standing on the aft end of the tug and we crashed into the pier and I went from one end of the deck to the other. That's how I got this scar and lost some of my teeth. I was only sixteen when I started and quite often I would be petrified and think I wouldn't see my mother again. When *The Stag* turned over on the Tyne around Swan Hunters, all the crew lost

52

their lives. The pilot had given orders to swing her around and the two tugs on the stern started to turn with the weight of the ship. As it got half way around the pilot told them to slacken down a bit and the two ropes went under the tug and just turned it over. The five crew went down with her.

Bill Salkeld

Take It Canny

I worked up and down the river as an arc welder and in later years for the Tyne Improvement Commission. The T.I.C., or 'take it canny' as we called it, was a non profit making organisation. The profits were all ploughed back into the organisation, but I never saw any of it.

During the war, Readheads could build, rivet and launch a ten thousand ton ship every six weeks. The men were on a lue rate, half-piece and half-time. It was always casual work in the dry dock. When the ship went out, if there wasn't another one due, you were out as well. No one was permanent unless they were a blue eye or a brown nosier. You could bet your bottom dollar that they would pay-off all of the casuals at Christmas because they didn't want to pay the holiday pay. The employers had it to a fine art, especially Smith Dock.

In 1944 there was only two arc welding firms on the Tyne, the Anglo Swedes and British Arc Welding. We had a religious foreman and he could never take a joke. If we got a bottle of something off the sailors he would never touch a drop. Readheads could have built the biggest ships on the Tyne, but their three births went straight into the river which didn't give a lot of clearance on the opposite bank.

When I worked for the T.I.C. one of my jobs was maintaining the steam crane on the end of south pier. It was used to drop ten and twenty ton blocks along the pier to protect it from the sea. The blocks were made in big cradles at the pier works from cement and clinker, loaded on to little wooden bolsters by a big Goliath crane and then a loco would push them out along the pier. Getting up top to make repairs was never a problem, but once you were there it was always cold even in the summer. You didn't wipe your nose, the wind blew it away. Although we stiffened it up as much as possible, the crane deteriorated with the wind and salt water and eventually Lloyds told the Port of Tyne Authorities that it was unsafe for load bearing and had to be condemned. The pier is always getting a pounding off the sea, and once you've got a little hole through, the pressure just strips everything away. A few years ago one part of the south pier was almost hollowed out and you could hear the tide sloshing about inside. We had to open it up and fill it with ready mix quick drying cement. In the latter years Alfie Damms ran the crane and drove the loco. A maintenance man performed the smaller repairs. He had a little cabin on wheels and Alfie used to push him up the pier in the mornings, leave him there to work and then fetch him back at night. The pier is almost a mile long so it would be too far to walk.

Jim Thompson

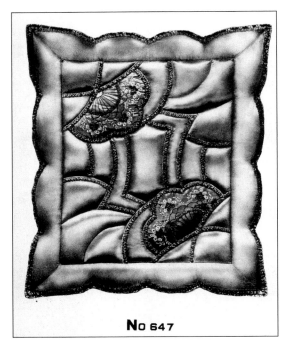

<No 647>

A CWS Pelaw down quilt designed by Joyce
Carlson in 1953.

'Oh No, Not A Quilt Designer!'

I won a five year scholarship to South
Shields Art Collage when I was
thirteen. But my parents wouldn't let
me go. They told me I had to get a
proper job. As it happened I was at the
art school one evening when the
headmaster Mr Gill came around and
asked if any of us wanted a job as a
designer at Pelaw Down Quilts for the
Co-operative Wholesale Society. I
thought, 'Oh no, not a quilt designer',
but my parents wanted me to go after
the job. I had an interview on a
Wednesday afternoon and started the
following Monday. I was there twelve
years. I've still got a few photographs of
the quilts I designed. Some of them are
now in the Shipley Museum.

Joyce Carlson

Busy at East Boldon

My first job was with British Rail
and I worked in a little wooden
hut in what was East Boldon goods
station. Everyone sent stuff by British
Rail in those days, so even at a place
like East Boldon we were always very
busy.

Colin Barnsley

The 8.02 From Tyne Dock

I used to get the 8.02 electric train from
Tyne Dock Station up go Pelaw.
There were lots of staff working on the
stations and there was a lovely waiting
room with a coal fire inside. Sometimes
we would see a dog or a cat walking
along the railway line and I watched
hoping they would move off the track. If
they touched the electric rail they
would jump up in the air screaming
with the shock. Once there was a dead
horse on the line just before Pelaw,
again because of the electric line. It
took a couple of men a good half hour
to get it off the track. When I got into
work I told the manager that I was late
because the train had to stop for a dead
horse. He though I was being cheeky.

Joyce Carlson

The Station Was Full

I started working at South Shields
station as a porter. When I arrived we
still had gas lamps in the station and the
carriages. In the storehouses they still
had the tin hot water bottles that the

South Shields Station staff in 1973. Left to right: Ronnie Stratford, J. Robson, Hilda Adie, Maisie Bell, W. Robertson and Willie Stott.

passengers used to rent from the porters to warm up their feet. They had not been used since the First World War. The place was full of posters for holiday resorts. I used to put them up and now I wish I had kept some because they are now worth a fortune. In the carriages were hand painted pictures of various parts of the country and they are now worth money as well. Then I became a shunter and I shunted a lot of famous trains and engines – *The Silver Link, Queen of the South, Heart of Midlothian, Sir Nigel Grersly*. They all came in at one time because Shields used to run main line excursions. There would be trains to Blackpool for miners' week and we used to get the mining villages coming in for their day trips. They

would bring their colliery band with them and march down Ocean Road with all their kids and families for a day at the beach. I left the station in 1959 just before Dr Beeching's axe started to fall on the railways.

John Tinmouth

Tickets And Parcels

When I stared at South Shields Station in 1963 we would open up the ticket office at 6.30 in the morning to take bookings. Sometimes, as I went to work, I could hear the hooters from the ships. The booking office was quite cosy. In winter we had a big coal fire burning all day. We would take bookings for the excursion trains that ran direct from South Shields to places like Glasgow, Edinburgh and Penzance. When the miners' holidays and the shipyard holidays were on in the summer we had queues running right outside of the station all the way down to the public toilets. Just working out the journey and the connections could take ages because the timetables were huge and quite complex. When I first started, the tickets were stored in alphabetical order and by price in a big ticket rack on the wall. Whenever the prices changed, we had to re-order the racks. Later on, we got a machine to print them up as we needed. We had to cope with everything – refunds, complaints and booking sleepers and seats from Newcastle. We could tell

whenever a ship had come in because there would be sailors coming up to the window with their travel warrants and we would issue them all tickets.

After about a year I became the senior clerk and I did the wages for the station staff and also for the signal box at Harton (Tyne Dock) and anyone who worked away, but wanted to pick up their pay at South Shields. They were all on my pay sheet. The platform staff congregated in a wooden shed beside the ticket barrier that we called the cabin. The chargeman, who was responsible for most of the day to day running of the platform, used to work from there and that was where they would do the hand over between the various duties.

When the Tyne Tunnel was opened by the Queen, the Royal Train came to

A Newcastle-bound DMU train in South Shields Station in 1978 shortly before closure. The wooden cabin is on the right next to the footbridge.

The station entrance the day after closure. The newsagents in the ticket hall remained open for some time to cater for passengers using the replacement bus service from Mile End Road.

Track removal at High Shields Station shortly after closure of the line to Newcastle. To allow construction of the Metro to begin, the track was singled between South Shields and Tyne Dock.

Jarrow Station. Most of the staff were issued with special tickets so they could stand on Jarrow platform to see her but I didn't get one. However, the Royal Train came down empty to Shields Station. I think it was so the engine could be turned. I can remember some of the staff being concerned because we hadn't used the turntable in years and there was some doubt that it would actually work on the day. When the train reached Shields, I went on to the platform to have a look at it and when I got closer I could see inside the carriage. There were cans of hair spray and cosmetics piled up on a table. I don't know if they belonged to the Queen or the ladies in waiting. When I went home that night I told my husband,

who was a strong union man, that I had touched the Royal Train. He was absolutely horrified I should be so excited by it. The next time I saw one of his friends he looked at me and laughed and asked if I had washed my hand yet.

There used to be a huge amount of parcel traffic through the station and late at night there would be a special train to take everything away. At Christmas we used to send off the Wright's Biscuits hampers. The company used to have a very good trade and we would work late into the night to get them all weighed, labelled and sent off. Each station in the county had its own number and we would stick the correct one on each hamper so they

58

would be put off at the right stop. Newman's, who made ladies lingerie, sent their parcels through us and we also handled heavy bits of precision machinery from the shipyards that needed to be sent off for repair.

There used to be a weighbridge just outside the parcels office. The package and the trolley would be weighed and the weight of the trolley subtracted to work out the weight to charge for. It was a very busy little parcels office. By the middle of the 1960s, the special trains were getting less and less, the direct service to Sunderland stopped and they hardly used the far side platform. When the paytrains came in and most of the other stations on the line closed down, we took over the parcel business from Jarrow and Hebburn. We used to have five motor vans out in the yard delivering parcels. In 1969, when the area management took over, the accounts went to Darlington, although we still sent the parcels off from Shields. They wouldn't spend any money on the station and gradually it became run down. The Finley's kiosk was frequented by all of the smokers on the staff as well as the passengers, but we could see their trade dying away.

My friend worked there, until one week she went away on holiday and when she came back and got off the train she found the company had taken the kiosk away. She said, 'Its just like Dr Who's Tardis has disappeared.' Then the station master went as well. All that was left was the ticket office staff. We were left to run the place by ourselves with only an area manager coming in every two weeks to check everything was running all right. We still sold tickets for excursions from Newcastle, but

unfortunately they would often leave quite early in the morning, sometimes before the connecting train from South Shields had arrived. We had to explain to the passengers quite carefully that although it might say from South Shields on the ticket, they would have to get the bus up as far as Newcastle if they were going to make the connection.

One day I was so fed up with the old paint I brought some emulsion to brighten up the booking office. I left the office shortly before the line closed to make way for the Metro. I enjoyed my time there and one of the things I liked most was when passengers came back from a holiday I had arranged some would tell me they had had a good time and thanked me. Some people even sent us post cards.

Maisie Bell

Hard and Heavy to Drive

In 1959 I became a trolley bus conductor for South Shields Corporation Transport. Later I went on the motor buses as a spare driver and after that an inspector. Trolley buses were magnificent things, fast and very economical but you couldn't weave in out of the traffic because you were restricted by the length of the trolley. The Criterion pub at the bottom of Purvis Street had a great big net slung across it because if the driver went too fast, the trolleys would come off and go straight through the pub window. Then the traffic would be stopped while the crew hooked them back on with thirty foot long poles. If you drove to the

Corporation and Northern bus crews in the Market Square. John Tinmouth is in the centre.

and some people wanted us to transport bags of coal. The only places you could have your break were Tyne Dock or the pier and then only three minutes. We all used to have bad stomachs because we had to eat so fast.

John Tinmouth

Privilege Tickets

My dad used to work for the LNER at Tyne Dock and we used to get privilege tickets. It was cheaper for us to travel on the train than the bus.

Jean Cockayne

market you had to take the trolley off the wire so the other buses could pass. Some drivers would forget and then another one would come along, run smack into it and the booms would break. The motor buses were hard and heavy to drive because they didn't have the power systems they have now. The reason we have an open top bus is because one was driven under a bridge in Victoria Road. They had taken the bridge down for repairs and of course they put it back and never told us. One of the lads drove around that way and took the top off the bus. Making it open top was the cheapest way of getting some use out of it. Once a women left a baby on the bus. A man once asked me if he could take an armchair on the bus

John Landells.

Colin and Freda Barnsley.

A Gentleman Of The Press

My first job was as an junior clerk with an accountant in Winchester Street in 1934. I was paid five shillings a week with one and tuppence taken off for insurance stamps. It doesn't sound much, but I was envied by all of my school leaving friends because I had a job and that was very important in the depression. Then the accountant went bankrupt after six weeks and I was out. I spent the next fourteen months trudging around shipyards and firms looking for work and getting the same reply, 'Sorry, no vacancies.' Then I did get a break as a junior-cum-messenger boy for an ageing senior partner in a firm of solicitors. He was bedridden and worked from home and I mainly trafficked between him and the office, again for five shillings a week. After eighteen months, the old man died and

I was redundant again. Then I got a job in Reyrolle at Hebburn in the solicitors office and also a Saturday afternoon job cycling around the area collecting half-time and then full time scores for the *Football Gazette*. This led me into journalism, which became my career. After the war I became shipping reporter for the *Shields Gazette*, writing about ship movements, ship orders and the strikes. When the yards were nationalised in 1977, I was head-hunted to become Chief Press Officer for British Shipbuilders in Newcastle. Looking back, I enjoyed my career.

John Landells

The Bank's Permission

I was working for Barclays Bank when I wanted to get married to Freda. It might sound strange now but I had to ask the bank's permission before we could go ahead with the wedding. In those days the banks had a set age of twenty-five at which they would allow their staff to get married and some of them were very strict about observing it as well. I had to go in and see the manager and say that Freda and I were thinking of getting married. Luckily they allowed it to happen when I was only twenty-four.

Colin Barnsley

Second Choice Of The Baths

The first job I had was in Byker, making Lone Ranger masks and Christmas cards. I was the only coloured lad there, and didn't have that many friends, so I used to stop on the job when other people were going for breaks. The boss thought, 'I have never had a worker like this', and he used to give me extra money in my pay packet. When I got a job on the buses the other staff used to take the mickey out of my turban, saying things like, 'I hope your head gets better soon', and that sort of thing. It was OK at first, but after a while it gave me a bad temper and I had to change my job. I got a job up at Hexham making coloured dyes. I had to leave home at seven o'clock and got back at ten, sometimes seven days a week. After a while we noticed that the coloured lads were on the machines with the dried dyes, which got dye all over you, but the English people were working with the wet dye and that wasn't so bad. On the night time there were only a certain number of baths and

all the English got the first choice of them and we came after. By that time it was too late because we had to go and catch the bus. So I said to the boss, 'There are some big drums downstairs we can fill them up with water, there is no shortage of hot water, and so we can have a bath.' So that was what we did to get home on time. In those days we couldn't always get jobs, so we had to take the good with the bad.

M.S. Shabilla

A Good Education

When I was at Ocean Road School in the 1950s we used to teach the children whose parents worked at the fairground. I can remember the head of the school trying to impress on the class how important it was to get a good education. One of the little boys from the fair put his hand up and said, 'No that's not right Sir. Mr So and So from the fair can't even write his own name properly and he is worth thousands.' The poor headmaster was so taken aback he didn't know what to say.

Ethel Dawson

Diving

My father was a diver and if the river was busy he used to keep me off school to turn the handle on the air pump. We were Thomas Keedy and Sons. I was diving when I was seventeen. When you went down, you used to see things lost overboard – fouled propellers, anchors and even bodies occasionally. Through working in it, I could never romanticise about the river. It was one of the dirtiest rivers in the world. It was amazing the things I used to find floating about. One day when I was doing a job there was a dead dog floating around me. I would give it a push with a pole and then go down under the water. When I came back up this dead dog would come bobbing back. One day, when at the Mill Dam, I dropped a bucket into the river to get some water to clean the decks. When I pulled it back up there was a dead baby inside. There used to be a lot of still births just dumped in the river.

I feel that our generation just survived and when people talk to me about the good old days I don't want to know. I hate it when people try to romanticise the past and the jobs we had to do. There may have been a community spirit but we didn't know anything else. I just think of the old fashioned middens, outside toilets, no baths, mattresses in the back lane, women in the back yards with their poss sticks and hands red raw from carbolic soda. The skin was often ripped off miners' backs by falls of coal.

There was nothing clever about having to go to work at six o'clock in the morning. I never saw my children through the hours I had to work. It was terrible, it was like going down to hell every day. If we had decent living wages we would never have had to work those long hours. In the old days you would always hear men saying things like, 'I'm never letting my son go down the mine or into the shipyards.'

Ernie Keedy

Ernie Keedy.

Low Wages

When they de-regulated the buses they finished everyone who was fifty years and over. Lads who had started off as point boys were paid off because the new company didn't want to pay the superannuation on their pensions. We finished under the PTE on the Saturday night, then on the Monday morning the company became Busways. They recruited about a hundred and twenty new drivers on new contracts, that kind of thing happened at bus depots all over.

John Tinmouth

A Volcano

Our ice cream has won awards from the trade association, the Ice

Cream Alliance. We came first in Europe for coffee ice cream. One year, I entered with an ice cream sundae I called Volcano. I made it in a big tall glass and started with cherries at the bottom for the Earth's core then mandarin pieces for the heat. Then came cinder toffee for the crust and I built up the outer core with mini marsh mallows and then chocolate ice cream for the Earth itself. To top it off I made a crater out of marsh mallow and put a sugar cube and some alcohol inside. I brought out a great big blow torch and the judges nearly died when I turned the torch on and the whole thing went whoosh right up in the air! This was to make the volcano erupt and toast the marshmallow. It was a great effect and a bold statement, but I came second. A girl from Northern Ireland won it with a basket of fruit.

Michael Minchella

The Keedy's diving boat. At the bottom left Ernie Keedy can be seen in a diving suit.

CHAPTER 4
Wartime

South Shields Station after an air raid on the night of 9 April 1941. In the same raid the Queen's Theatre was destroyed. (Courtesy South Tyneside Libraries)

Three 'C' class submarines moored to a quay near The Groyne. (Courtesy Beamish Museum)

The Zeppelin

During the Great War I can remember my father picking me out of my cot and taking me to the top of Imeary Street to watch the Zeppelin come over Westoe Village. It dropped a bomb near Murphy's Fair, down where Burstro's was beside the market. My father must have been crackers. He was holding me up to see the Zeppelin while there were bombs falling all around us.

Ernie Keedy

Four Pounds A Week

During the First World War some of the younger women came into their own when they got jobs working in the munitions factories. They discovered what they could do and that they were actually intelligent. They were earning four pounds a week which was a fortune.

Some of the older people were scandalised by this because the girls were going out and buying fur coats with the money. The girls thought that this life was going to continue after the war but when the men came home they found that they were catapulted straight back into domestic service.

Jean Shanahan

Vickers Armstrong

My mother, was born in 1895 around Tyne Dock. When the First World War started she went to work at the munitions factory at Vickers Armstrong. One day she brought a shell casing home and we used it to keep our poker in it.

Edith Atkinson

When The Town Hall Clock Struck Eleven

Just before the war my father had an uncle who lived in Prince Edward Road which then was the back of beyond. Every Sunday we would get the tramcar from Chichester to visit him. There used to be a tiny little tobacconists there and before getting on the tram my dad would take me and my sister inside and buy us some sweets. My favourite was Palm Toffees Banana Splits. Then we would wait for the first car, which always came out of the sheds just after the stroke of eleven because on Sundays the service didn't start running until then. On 3 September 1939 Neville Chamberlain had said that unless we heard from Hitler by eleven, then we would be at war. That day when we heard the town hall clock striking eleven we just looked at each other and forgot about the tram and went home. I was just a boy and I remember thinking, great there is going to be a war. Later on, when they built the anti-tank trap at Chichester, the tobacconists almost disappeared behind it.

Tom Dawson

The Significance Or The Danger

The very first time the sirens went I was with my friend buying some sweets at a little shop called Bennett's in Park Avenue. They always had a lovely display and we became too absorbed in choosing from it to be interested in the wailing noise around us. Being so young

Isaac Wilkinson in First World War uniform.

we didn't realise the significance or the danger of what we were hearing.

Kathleen Burdon

Arrested And Interned

In the First World War Italy was on the British side and the immigrant population was given the choice of either joining a regiment over here or one back in their own home country. If you joined a British regiment you were given British citizenship on your discharge. Joe, my grandfather, didn't take advantage of this and at the start of the Second World War he was still an Italian citizen. He was arrested and interned. They took all of the Italians in

Bomb damage to the YMCA field and Lisle Road houses, 25 April 1941.

South Shields down on to the north pier. They were there for one night and then Joe was sent to Bishop Auckland. Strangely, he was allowed back to Shields at the weekend. They didn't seem to be so hard on the Italians in South Shields as they were in other places. In Sunderland the Notiarianni's were sitting in their shop when the police broke the doors down and arrested them. Even allowing for war time animosity this was going too far.

Michael Minchella

Evacuated

For the first four years of the war I was evacuated to Appleby and this was the first holiday I ever really had.

John Irwin

Into The Air Raid Shelter.

When I started school, the war was on. We were given a tin mug and a packet of biscuits and we had to take them down into the air raid shelter. We were told they were in case we were ever stuck inside for any length of time. We were shown where we would each have to sit if there was an air raid. Because of the war the classrooms were really overcrowded. Sometimes there were sixty pupils in each class, but the teachers could still keep control of the children. There were a lot of problems caused by the war but the teachers were all really dedicated to the pupils. Sometimes if they were really short of staff we would just go in the mornings or just the afternoons.

Mary Peterson

At school we were issued with emergency food rations but we quite often ate them in the yard. So if we had been trapped in the shelter we would have starved.

Ethel Dawson

Try To Get Home

An air raid started just when we were leaving school. One of the teachers said to me, 'You can come in the school shelter or you can try to get home.' Fancy saying that to a child. I remember going part of the way home then just getting so terrified and cowering against the railings. Our Norma came to collect me and she had a coat on her head as if that would do any good.

Mary Peterson

If there was an air raid on during the night and it lasted until midnight, you didn't start school until ten o'clock in the morning. If it lasted until after two o'clock in the morning we didn't have to go in until the afternoon. We used to pray they would last until two.

Tom Dawson

Gas Masks

We used to have to take our gas masks to school. Everyone was checked as you went into the class room and if you didn't have one you were sent straight home. I would feel sick when I put the mask on.

Mary Peterson

Hot Shrapnel

I would be late getting to school if there had been a raid the night before because I used to pick up the shrapnel on the High Road on my way in. The shrapnel was still hot. The bomb I experienced first hand was a land mine that was dropped beside the YMCA building at the back of the High School. It was so powerful that it blew everything in the shelter forwards and we were all lifted up with the force of it. It almost destroyed the YMCA.

Bill Salkeld

The First In Our Street

Our air raid shelter was the first in our street to be built. The men from the council came along and erected four columns of bricks in the

Colin and Ken Barnsley, 1938.

back yard and put a concrete slab on top which rested half on the toilet and half on the wash-house. The three of us were down there during the heaviest raids. Then an official from the town hall came along to check on the construction and told us it was a death trap. If the house had fallen down the cement block would have fallen on us. After building our shelter, the workmen had realised it was unsafe and although they hadn't built any more like it, they didn't bother to tell us it was defective. My mother went mad when she found out about it. We started using a neighbour's shelter at the other side of the back lane. Our neighbour's daughter, Meggey never got up for the air raids, she just stayed in the house. Whenever there was a raid on the mother was always sitting inside the shelter saying, 'Oh my God. Oh my God', over and over again. I used to wish she would shut up. Then she would shout, 'Meggy! Meggy! Are you getting up, come out here.' Meggy would shout back, 'Oh shut up mother.' I was about twelve and didn't realise how serious the war was. I use to think she was making a fuss over nothing.

Joyce Carlson

They dug a big hole in our garden and put the Anderson Shelter in there. We had to climb down steps to get inside. We had a hole in the roof and my brother Ken and I put a tube through it to try and spot enemy aircraft as they were overhead. Sometimes we used to go in the cupboard under the stairs. It was warmer than going out of the house and the protection was just as good.

Colin Barnsley

Blown Into The Shelter

Every time there was an air raid my dad would throw a coat over my head and between the flashes of the gunfire we would dash up to the top of the garden and dive into the shelter. I can't remember being frightened. I would go to sleep in the shelter and when I woke up I would be back in the house in my parent's bed. When the land mine dropped in the bottom of Lisle Road there were a couple of people killed. My dad was outside at the time and he was blown into the shelter. When the raid was over and we went back into the house there was soot all over. One morning the shelter was full of water so after that we had to use the one across the road. If you didn't have room in the back yard, you didn't have a shelter, just a steel cage under the table which you had to climb inside. I think the council made the steel bars for them.

Mary Peterson

ARP Duty

I was based at the ARP Post at what is now McAnany Avenue. One night I had to take a message to the next post at Harton Village during a heavy raid. I remember cycling along Harton Lane in the dark and the anti-aircraft guns were firing and the shrapnel was coming down and hitting the road ahead of me and sparks were shooting up. I was wearing my tin hat. For someone who was fourteen-years-old it was an exciting experience. The next morning I would go to school trying to find shrapnel for souvenirs.

Ken Corner

My dad, Robert Gill, was a miner and also an air raid warden. There was a plaque on the front of our house to tell people they could come to him for help. I don't know how he managed all those shifts at the pit.

Mary Peterson

The Coal Had To Be Shipped

When the bombs dropped around Chichester Road they blew about 200 yards of the coal train track to hell. There was chunks of railway line found 300 yards away in Randel Street embedded in people's roofs. But the coal still had to be shipped and we had to get the track repaired. They had the men from the pit shovelling like mad to fill in the crater. They threw in bricks from the surrounding bomb damaged buildings, everything they could get their hands on, even bits of furniture was used to get that hole filled in. We had it all put back in twelve hours.

Bill Henderson Snr

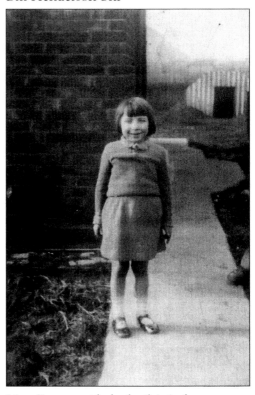

Mary Peterson with the family's Anderson Shelter.

Fire Watching

The men at Readheads Shipyard used to do fire watching duty after work and sometimes my father used to stay out almost all night. My father used to play the concertina and sometimes he would take it along to entertain the rest of the men

Ethel Dawson

I used to fire watch at King Street. There was a bed in the office where I worked and when you looked out the window late at night you would see some sights in the street below. There were often ladies of the night walking around King Street with sailors in uniform. Their nationality varied as different boats came into the Tyne.

Ken Corner

Incendiary Bombs

They dropped a lot of incendiary bombs on Brinkburn playing fields. Just after one raid, three of us went down there with the bogie. We found a bomb that hadn't exploded and we picked it up and put it on the bogie. Ignorance is bliss! We were coming up Mortimer Road and got to the junction of Birchington Avenue and Oxford Street and there was a copper there. As soon as he saw what we had he shouted out, 'Where do you think your going with that lot?' and he came racing over. We just looked at him and told him we were taking it home.

Tom Dawson

When we were in the Anderson Shelter behind our house in Harton House Road we could hear the bombs coming down. Everyone in the street had clubbed together to buy bits of emergency equipment and everyone had been allotted a job. Mr Walker and I went running up and down with a pair of ladders and a set of pails putting the fire bombs out. We were in the shelter around midnight when we heard wardens banging on the door. They told us a bomb had hit the corner of the house over the road and landed in the kitchen. Fortunately it hadn't exploded but we all had to leave the street at once. Everybody was in a panic about what to do and where to go. The lady next door, Mrs Brown, had a sister in Marsden Road beside the Co-op Store and she let me and my parents stay there until morning. We sat up all night in chairs trying to get to sleep. For me it was very worrying, but at the same time a very exciting experience. The next morning there was rope stretched across the end of Harton House Road and a policeman standing by it. He wouldn't let us go back to the house, even just to get something to wear. We were just in our siren suits and we had to borrow clothes. I went off to Stafford's the hairdressers where I worked and my mam went through to Sunderland to see if she could stay at my aunt's. At dinner time I tried to get into the house but the police wouldn't let me. The next day I went back again and the police escorted me into the house for just long enough to grab a few clothes for me and my mam. Two days later the bomb was cleared and we were allowed back.

Reta Emery

An unexploded bomb being removed from Harton House Road after being defused on 10 April 1941.

The *Namdo* moored in the Tyne. Built in Middlesbrough in 1907, it hit a mine in the North Sea in 1944. Ernie Keedy is on the left inside the divers launch.

Trevor Tate

I remember a boy called Trevor Tate who was a family friend. He was called up for the air force in 1942 when he was eighteen. He was taken prisoner by the Japanese. He was put on the Burma Railway and was among the prisoners who died out there. His mother was never the same again.

Joyce Carlson

Divers To The Navy

We were official divers to the navy during the war. We were sworn in at Clifford Fort at the bottom end of the fish quay. When the war started everyone was edgy about missiles and shells being lost overboard. Once I went down below and after a while I felt a pull on the line for me to come up. That was unusual because they were normally be happy to let you stay down for as long as possible. When I got up I found that there was an air raid going on. I had to clamber out of my boots and then run for the shelter and sit there in this thick diving suit in the heat amongst a crowd of women workers from the nearby factory. Another time, we were called to a mooring stage at the bottom of the fish quay gut and told a depth charge had exploded during the night and a boat had gone to the bottom. I went down and found just a few ribs and planks from this ship. I came up and recorded what I had found. Then I was told that there had been two ratings on board when the charge had gone off. I went down again looking for two bodies, but really you don't want to find those. I didn't find anything and later on it

transpired that the ratings who were supposed to be guarding the ship hadn't been on board at all. They had been ashore with two ladies of the night and didn't know how to explain their survival. So in one way it turned out all right.

Ernie Keedy

I remember HMS *Lweander* coming in to Tyne Dock after she had been torpedoed. My father took me down to see her and the hole in the side was so big you could have driven a bus through it.

John Tinmouth

Olga Carlson.

Mary Peterson with her father, Robert Edward Gill, in the early years of the Second World War.

Rationing

During the war the pork shops like Dickson's weren't as rationed as most of the other food shops and they were often open until ten o'clock at night. My grandfather was very fond of saveloy dip for his supper and I would be sent out to the shop at Park Avenue. The black out was on and me and my aunt would be sent up the road with a tiny torch with a very thin beam. All you could do was shine it down, to try to pick out the pavement and you couldn't see a thing in front of you.

Ethel Dawson

In the war there was one butcher's shop in Green Street that always had mince pies in stock. There were a lot of stories, which I'm not going to repeat here, about where he got the meat from, but we still used to queue up to buy his pies all the same.

Olga Carlson

I use to like the dried egg. It was quite nice really. We used to eat it fried. There was a brown flour called National Flour that had the husks and grains left in for our health. But everyone thought that white bread was the best and my mother used to sieve them all out with a big dish and a cloth and we used to feed the husks to our hens at the allotment. You didn't let people know what you were doing because it was against the law. I don't think we had heard about vitamins. Cakes were in short supply. We only got them about once a week maybe with some kind of imitation cream. We had to stand in a queue and pick our cakes from a big wooden tray. My mother always took the plain ones with maybe a few currents in and leave the best ones. She said she didn't like to look greedy, but I would go mad with her for not choosing some good ones.

Joyce Carlson

Pushing In

On the corner of the Nook there was a butchers, a bakers and a grocers. You used to have to queue for hours at each. My mother used to say to me, 'You stand in that queue', while she went to another shop. Then she would come and take my place. I used to die of shame. Other people would say, 'Look at her, she's pushing in.' I know other people used to do it, but at the time I felt like it was only me. I used to hate it. My mother used to drag me everywhere to stand in queues.

Mary Peterson

We used to cry when we couldn't have sweets.

Bill Salkeld

Black Market Ice Cream

During the war my father, Fred, was a Bevin boy and he somehow managed to keep the ice cream business going as well. Officially you couldn't make ice cream during the war because you weren't supposed to be able to get the ingredients, but there was still a demand for it and people found ways of

Bomb damage to Sea Road, 2 October 1941. (Courtesy South Tyneside Libraries)

getting ingredients on the black market. There was an ice cream substitute called Nu-Cream on the market which my father, along with others I might add, claimed to have invented. On the night the Market Square was bombed our shop in King Street was also destroyed. Fortunately, very shortly afterwards, they were able to buy the shop in Ocean Road which had also been an ice cream shop. We've been here ever since and have never looked back.

Michael Minchella

Carbide Crystals

The winter of 1941 was really severe and the emergency water reservoir near Laygate Lane froze over. Me and my three mates filled a lemonade bottle full of water and then put carbide crystals inside and they started to fizz. The crystals were supposed to be dropped into water to make gas for emergency lighting. We corked the bottle, made a hole in the ice and dropped it in the reservoir. Then we waited to see what would happen. After a period of time there was a terrific boom and ice scattered all over the place. There was a little old woman coming along the back lane of Dacre Street just as this thing went up and she flung her shopping bag up in the air and shouted, 'The bloody Germans are coming, the Germans are coming.'

Tom Dawson

The gas bus in the Market Square. (Courtesy South Tyneside Libraries)

Gas Bus

There used to be a bus service down Highfield Drive and up Harton Rise to Marsden Road. During the war they tried putting the gas powered buses on the route but the big bag on top would catch in the trees and they would rip holes in it.

Ethel Dawson

My Uncle Charlie's cousin was killed by a bomb up on King George Road. The family had come from London to escape the Blitz.

Joyce Carlson

Bullet Holes In The Lamp Post

The beaches, the open air swimming pool on the south foreshore and the row of shops above the North Marine Park were all closed off with barbed wire until the end of the war. There was an anti-aircraft gun and searchlight at the bottom of Prince Edward Road, down in the hollow where the houses are now. A land mine dropped on the corner of Lascelles Avenue and King George Road killed a family that came up from London to escape the Blitz. There was also a big crater at the top of Centenary Avenue where a bomb had dropped. One bomb even came down in Harton Cemetery and exploded among the graves. There was bits of bodies lying everywhere amongst the houses and they got the lads from the pits to pick up the bits. When the bombs hit the market place, we all came down from school to see the damage that had been done. There were bullet holes in the lamp post opposite Franchies. They were there until very recently. Theatres and public buildings like The Palladium were always sand bagged in case of bomb damage. At night it was pitch dark because of the black out but when a raid started you could suddenly see everything because the searchlights were on.

John Tinmouth

Guards and Barbed Wire

After the market was bombed all of Commercial Road was barred off to keep people out of the area. Being a young boy, and not being interested by guards and barb wire, I went through the churchyard to have a look at the damage. I saw all the turmoil – buses upside down with ambulances and the army all around the square. That sight has always stayed with me.

Alfred Beris

The German Parachutist

We got out the shelter in Borough Road and watched a German parachutist come down beside the Marine Park. That was a brilliant moonlit night. The place was lit up with searchlights and he drifted down and got caught in the telephone wires. He was all right, though at the time some of us wanted to kill him.

John Tinmouth

There were Italian prisoners of war held in what used to be the police station beside Prince Edward Road at the Nook. Its a flower shop now. Me and my father were walking down Borough Road when we saw one of the neighbours with two men. I remember thinking they were talking in a funny language. My father told me they were 'Ities'.

Bill Salkeld

Knees Up At The Nook

We had two Canadian airmen lodging with us because their barracks were always freezing and they used to lodge out if they could. Even though I was quite young I used to think of them as being quite handsome. A lot of people had a good time during the war because the place was full of servicemen. They always used to have a good knees up at the Nook. The pubs were always full.

Mary Peterson

Cockroaches Crawl Out

My brother Albert had only been at sea a few months when the Second World War started. We never knew when he was going to come home. He was torpedoed three times and once turned up in the middle of the night wearing an old pair of shoes and old

Albert Wilkinson in 1942, aged 18.

jacket and trousers. The sleeves of the jacket were half way up his arms. Sometimes when he came home he used to stand his suitcase in the hearth. When he opened it loads of cockroaches would crawl out and we had to sweep them into the fire.

Joyce Carlson

Cardboard Medals

We were given cardboard medals according to how much paper and cardboard we could save. If you collected so much you were given a medal with sergeant on. If you collected even more paper you became a staff sergeant or a major if you were a real high achiever.

Colin Barnsley

Woollen Blankets.

In their spare time at school the girls used to knit woollen blankets. I think they were for the soldiers. When one of our teachers, Wallice Coxson, was on yard duty he would walk around knitting a blanket – a whole blanket. He was a one off!

Ethel Dawson

Play Hell With The Tailors

During the war I was a designer at Pelaw Quilts. We could still make things like embroidered quilts and baby's bibs and cushion covers but the designs had to be very restricted. It was more difficult to do lots of cheap designs than it was to design more expensive things.

I think a lot of fashions died out during the war. Turn-ups on trousers disappeared then. Then waistcoats became scarce. I think that is why they went out of fashion. As far as I remember there were still school uniforms during the war, but you couldn't be made to wear them if you didn't have them. Gradually the children were allowed to stop wearing caps and ties. Of course school trousers were all short trousers then.

Joyce Carlson

Material For Shorts

Because of the war it was only in my last few years at school that we could start to play sport. The first time we were able to organise a proper school football team you couldn't get football strips or shorts. So the teachers got hold of a pile of old blackout curtains and, with a pattern, cut out sections of material. We got two bits of material each to take home and then our mothers had to sew them together to make a pair of shorts. I was lucky that the son of a woman over the road had just left school and I got his football boots. During the war you were someone if you had a pair of football boots.

John Tinmouth

The Redifusion Box

During the war we all used to hang around the Redifusion box. Compared with the radio, it was very easy to use. Just one big switch that used to clunk around the channels – one, two, three. I can remember being sick of the news at one o'clock. I used to think that when the war was over there would never be any news again and I felt disappointed when it just kept going.

Mary Peterson

First Boys Back

When it was announced they were opening up the pier again our teacher told us we could get out of school an hour early if we went down to watch. I was one of the first ten boys in Shields to go back along the pier and I haven't been back since.

Alfred Beris

Tragic News

There was a lady called Mrs Barker who lived two doors away. She had two sons who died in prisoner of war camps in Germany. On Victory Night she was icing a victory cake when two policemen arrived and told her that her thirteen-year-old son Dennis just had been killed. He had been playing with a friend and they had come across a cartridge and had taken it into a garden shed. The other boy had gone out of the shed and Dennis was left tampering with the cartridge. It exploded and killed him outright. The shock of what had happened was so great for Mrs Barker that it didn't sink in for a while. She calmly asked my mother if she wouldn't mind finishing icing the victory cake and went with the policeman to the station. When she went away my mother started shaking.

Kathleen Burdon

The 8th Durham Battn South Shields Home Guard.

A London Transport bus on loan to South Shields Corporation Transport during the Second World War.
(Courtesy South Tyneside Libraries)

CHAPTER 5
People and Places

Minchella and Co. Ice Cream Parlour in Ocean
Road.

The Saturday Market

In the 1920s and '30s, the Saturday Market kept going until around nine o'clock at night. In the winter the stalls were lit by spluttering and hissing carbide lamps. Fridges and freezers were hardly heard of and on the meat and fruiterers' stalls everything had to be sold by the end of the day. In the last hour of the market, bargain hunters abounded.

John Landells

If you went down the market late at night you could smell the paraffin from the overhead lamps. People used to bake their own bread and brought it to sell. A man called Harry Randel used to make and sell toffee and toffee apples. Harry once gave me a pound note and asked me to run across to a shop and get him change. It was quite trusting of him because that was lot of money in those days.

Isabella Myers

Cure For All

In the market there was a man who had a very hoarse voice and always wore a white muffler. He used to sell chocolate for a shilling a bag if you could afford it. He also sold walnut whips. Anther man sold magic pads for half a crown each. He was there most weeks. There was a bump in the middle of them and he said they were a cure for all ailments and could clean clothes. Anything could be done with this pad. I was standing beside his stall and suddenly this other man came up and shouted out, 'Hey, I bought these off you the other day and I want my money back.' He was holding up a couple of the pads. He had opened up one of them and found that the bump was just full of sawdust. This was supposed to be the magic bit. He was shouting 'I want my money back' at the seller who was shouting back 'shut up' as he tried to unload the rest of his stock. Someone else used to sell pills that turned out to be sugar coated rabbit's dirt.

Ernie Keedy

Drunks Around The Market

The pubs around the market would have beer set up on the bar in advance for the men who worked by the river. When they came off shift it would be waiting for them and there would soon be quite a few drunks around the area.

My grandmother had to fend for herself after her husband died. She used to wear a shawl and a man's cap and took in washing and did other people's decorating so she was frightened of nobody. If she got to the market and saw men abusing their wives and rolling around drunk she used to lay into them and tell them to get home. The men got paid on Saturday nights and would go straight to the pub and the wives had to wait in the house and see how much money the men had when they got home.

Ethel Dawson

84

Dora Smith with the 1920s look of bobbed hair and fox fur.

I think the first shop in Shields that sold real Indian curry powder and spices was in the market. I used to go in there when I was about seventeen and at that time I had never tasted anything like it.

Hugh Amess

Illegal Gambling

When I was about eleven-years-old I was a bit of a gambler and I put sixpence each way on three horses. In those days gambling wasn't as tightly regulated as it was now, in fact there used to be bookies' runners all over the town. Wherever you were, if you wanted to put a bet on, you always knew a place close at hand where you could go. I went into this house in Saville Street which I knew was a place you could go to. When I checked the results in the paper at about half past four I found that I was one shilling to the good – which was a lot of money. I was over the moon but in the stop press in the same paper I found that the police had raided the house in Saville Street and taken the bookie. All the bets were confiscated so I got nothing back.

Terry Killen

The bookies' runners used to stand outside the pub which is now called

Styles of 1933. Leonard Edminson.

Burstro's Services walk round shop in Kepple Street. (Courtesy Beamish Museum)

the Royal Grill. One of the mothers in the area was a well known bookie's runner and whenever the police walked along the road she disappeared very fast.

Ethel Dawson

You could buy parcels of fish at the quay in South Shields. It was a bit like buying a pig in poke because they would never let you know what you were getting until after you had bought it.

Ken Barnsley

We used to go upstairs to the cafe at Binns and at the weekend they had an orchestra playing while you were having coffee.

Jean Cockayne

Billy Meths

When Billy Meths wasn't drunk he was a really intelligent man. He always used to sleep in the old lifeboat. He had another down and out in there with him and he used to charge him rent. He would often sleep on the bench beside Dickson's the pork shop at the bottom of Fowler Street. They found him dead in one of the churchyards. After he died, the rumour was that he was a naval officer from a very wealthy family in Liverpool.

John Tinmouth

Several well to do pensioners were sitting on a seat waiting for a bus. Billy Meths came along with his bottle of cider and his coat over his arm and said to them, 'Come on, you've got homes to go to, I haven't and your sitting on my bed.' They were so taken aback, they jumped up and he sat down. He took his shoes off and put them beneath the seat. Then he took his jacket off and folded it up for a pillow, lay on it and pulled his big coat over him. Finally he took a swig from the bottle, put it beneath the seat and went to sleep.

Joyce Carlson

T. Archer Lee

For three months during the war, I worked at T. Archer Lee the moneylenders. They were in an office on the corner of Charlotte Street just across the road from the Town Hall. I made the tea at ten and three and paid in money from the clients. Sometimes people would overpay and that went into the overpayments book in green ink, the bad debt was in another in red. We each had to bring in an attache case in the morning to take ledgers home at night in case the office was bombed.

Joyce Carlson

Escape From The Slaughterhouse

One day a bull escaped from the slaughterhouse and ended up in the station. I think it came down Station Road, past St Hilda's church yard, across the Market Square to Thrift Street and then past Wardles the saw mill and in

Tramcar No. 24 passing the T. Archer Lee building in Fowler Street. (Courtesy South Tyneside Libraries)

through Brighams gate. It managed to get on to the railway beside the turntable under River Drive. I was working at the parcels office and looked out of the window to see it in the yard leaping and snorting around. Then the police turned up along with the staff from the slaughterhouse who still had blood on their aprons. When I saw that I could understand why the animal wanted to get away. Then someone must have had a brainwave because they released some heifers and the bull calmed down, and followed them all the way back to the slaughterhouse.

Maisie Bell

Station Taxis

As well as running taxis, Station Taxis once used to offer horse drawn funerals. The stables used to be where Oz nightclub is now. The taxi part of the company has always been at the site on the station forecourt although there has been a series of different offices. One of the previous buildings was a converted beach hut. It was on wheels and in the late 1950s, when they tried to knock it down, it rolled off along Mile End Road. After that there was the old converted port cabin and that survived for about thirty years before the new building was put up. John Brown owned the company in the 1950s, he later went on to run Catch a Bus. My father took it over

Carbro Motors, Maxwell Street.

An advertisement card for Station Taxis.

from him in about 1975. The funeral side kept going until quite recently. It was just run as part of the taxi company which people would find strange. It was run out of Carbro Motors at Maxwell Street and it wasn't unknown for a body to spend the night there inside a hearse. Taxis were a different business to what they are now. The drivers were often ex-chauffeurs, and taxi and funerals duties used to be interchangeable. What job you were sent out on just depended where you were sitting in the queue of drivers. As well as funerals we used to carry the Mayor and we still carry the ballot boxes for the local and general elections. We used to have the black London style taxis but they had to be run as private hire cars which couldn't be flagged down in the streets and eventually they were to expensive to keep on. They were quite strong vehicles. I've been told that one winter somebody built a snowman and for some reason one of the drivers decided he was going to knock it down with his cab. However, it had been build around a concrete bollard and when he hit it the cab was totally wrecked. The drivers were paid on a mileage basis, their share was a third of the overall takings and there are stories of drivers reversing to Shields from Whitburn in order to re-wind the meter. If a driver was out for an unusual amount of time, after dropping off a customer, it wasn't unusual to find him in a lay-by with the meter in pieces trying to wind it back.

Paul Grey

Ocean Road in the late 1950s, viewed from the entrance to the South Marine Park.

She Liked Our Fire

An old woman always used to come to the train station and sit in the waiting room at night. Sometimes we used to try to get her into an old folks home or into care but she would only stay there for so long and then she would be back. I think she liked our fire. Once the Paytrains came, the waiting room closed and I never saw her after that.

Maisie Bell

It Meant Money

John Clay Street, Ada Street, George Potts Street and Stevenson Street were some of the most prosperous in the town. There was a shop on every corner and you could tell that it meant money was there. Although the people around there probably didn't get a lot of money, they were in work and that was important.

Ernie Keedy

The Store Man

People would get their grocery orders from the Co-operative Wholesale Society Store and Arthur was our store man. His wife had been ill in a flue epidemic. She recovered but went out of the house before she was completely better. She took the ferry over to North

Shields to see her family and she caught pneumonia and died. Arthur was absolutely devastated. After that, he became our lodger.

Joyce Carlson

The Crane

The big old crane on the pier used to fascinate me. We walked along the pier on a Sunday and I was always a bit scared walking under it because it was almost like walking into a dark cold pit. As you walked under the jib there was always the sound of metal creaking and groaning above you and once you got underneath there seemed to be huge amounts of wheels and pistons stretching down around you and they were covered in thick industrial grease. There were rails sunk into the stone at each side of the pier although the ones on the right hand side were actually several feet higher than those on the left because they were raised up on the sea wall. The rails ran back along the pier to a point about half way along. That was where the crane was secured and as far in as it could travel, but I don't think I ever saw it move. I remember thinking it was almost as if it was exiled from the town.

Jerimia Cornelius

Uncle George

My Uncle George was a nice person and a bit of a charmer. He was sea captain and with his personality and the money he earned he attracted many women. He was finally married at the age of thirty-five to a nurse by the name

The Tyne Improvement Commission crane. The train towards the end of the pier is carrying limestone blocks. (Newcastle City Libraries)

Uncle George.

of Bell. She met George when a friend asked him to take her to a hospital dance because he would be out of town on his own ship at the time. They kept in touch after the dance and finally nurse Bell went to visit him on his ship in Cardiff. One night she had been aboard and couldn't get back down the rope ladder. That was when he decided to buy her a ring and they were married a short while later.

Jean Shanahan

I used to go swimming every day in the bay up beside the pier. A friend of mine swallowed some sea water around there and, although he had never been ill in his life, he died about two weeks later. I don't suppose the sewage outlets went out as far as they do now and on his deathbed he swore it must have been something in the water he swallowed. He was in charge of the maintenance of the coast guard building at the pier head. The windows were probably the first double glazed windows in Shields. They were made by individually fixing in two sheets separated by a thin layer of air to keep the glass clear on stormy days. One day he asked me to go right up the top of the old coast guard pole beside the building, just to check that everything was secure. It had not been used in years but from the top of that you got a marvellous view of the town.

Ken Barnsley

Nurse Bell.

Frankie's cafe, 1982.

The Little Railway To The Pier

A lot of the stone for the pier came from the quarry at Trow Rocks, although it was used to break the force of the sea rather than in the construction of the pier itself. There was a little railway running from Trow Rocks to the pier and when it wasn't working we used to play on the trucks. We would bowl them along the lines and how we didn't get caught I don't know.

Ernie Keedy

The rolling stock from the Trow Rocks railway was kept locked up in the blockyard at the pier head and I used to strain to look through the gaps in the wooden fence to see what was inside. Sometime a little diesel would come out pushing a couple of wagons.

There was a guard's van that looked like a garden shed fixed on top of a flat wagon. By the 1970s the line was very rarely used. The sidings at the blockyard became very overgrown and then one year the whole lot was swept away to make a coach park.

Jerimia Cornelius

The Moustache

Harry Frankie had a long grey moustache, and always had a cigarette jammed in the corner of his mouth. Sometimes you could see where it had got too close and burnt a hole in his moustache.

Michael Minchella

The South Shields Corporation's water tram in the snow. (Courtesy South Tyneside Libraries)

Pullman Comfort

In the late 1920s South Shields Corporation Transport Department ran an advert extolling the virtue of the trams. Travel in 'Pullman Comfort' it said, which somehow did not apply on the top deck of a tram rattling and shaking its way down Hudson Street bank at Tyne Dock. Some of the cars had names like, 'Monarch of Bermuda', 'Caer Urfa' and 'Nelson'.

John Landells

Trams For The Rich, and Poor

I could tell where the trams were going to by the noise they made coming up Westoe Lane past the infirmary. The Tyne Dock trams were the rattley ones for the lower class people. The nicer trams were for Stanhope Road and the posh trams were for King George Road, where the councillors lived. You didn't hear the posh ones coming, they were so quiet, but the Tyne Dock trams could be heard coming up that bank for miles. A favourite tram of mine was the water tram. It was little more than a water tank on wheels and on hot days you would see it running around the main routes spraying water on to the cobbles. When I was a lad, my mates and I would run along behind it getting soaked.

Ernie Keedy

Tram at The Ridgeway in 1946. This is possibly the last tram to run in South Shields.

Laygate Flats

One of my friends called Ken lived on the third floor of the Laygate Flats and to me that was the poshest area in town. You went in and there was wall to wall carpet and it was always warm because they had central heating built in and they had a fantastic view out of the living room window.

Malcolm Grady

Green Street.

There was always something going on around Green Street. The slaughterhouse was at the end of the road and the cattle and sheep would sometimes escape and you would see the slaughtermen running up the road after them. There was a shop there called Moats that used to sell beautiful pies and pasties. They even used to sell jam pasties and they were great.

Hugh Amess

Porretas

Meeting at Porretas ice cream parlour in Frederick Street was the high spot of the weekend. We sat on the high stools, in little cubicles with long thin shelves, and ate ice cream with strawberry sauce and nuts. If we had the money we would play music on the juke box. We would buy records from a place

Lillian Thompson, wife of Hugh Amess, outside Meldon Terrace, Dean Road in 1961.

just around the corner called The Handy Shop. That was a great shop for us because they sold such a wide range of music.

Malcolm Grady

Full Make Up

On the opposite side of the back lane there was a house where, when the wife went out, the husband got dressed up in her clothes. I remember him wearing this white satin blouse and full make up with bright red lipstick and a silk scarf tied around his head just like a turban. Sometimes he would sit in the back yard, but often he would clean the back windows from the inside very

slowly. I think he was hoping people would see him, but no one used to talk about it. In those days it was unheard of, if not illegal, for a man to dress up in woman's clothes if he wasn't on the stage. His side of the lane used to get the sun in summer and he used to sit in his back yard in a deck chair with the door wide open wearing a flowered dress, high heels, a big straw hat and earrings. He would sit reading. One woman did mention what he did to his wife but she just denied it. In those days I don't suppose she could do anything else. I heard stories that he had gone out in her clothes and had been arrested twice. When he got older and became infirm, she used to bring him out into the back yard wearing her clothes, and she would just leave him in the deckchair in the strong sunlight. He used to look like he was exhausted with heat stroke, but he couldn't move and just sat there slumped and sweating with the lipstick and mascara running down his face. We could see him through the open back door and felt sorry for him, but some how none of us wanted to go over and say anything. It felt like we were intruding on some public, but unmentionable secret.

Joyce Carlson

Porky Martin's

We used to go to Porky Martin's the pork butchers on Stanhope Road on a Saturday and get a big jug of hot peas in OXO and sometimes with a saveloy.

Olga Carlson

My Uncle Jacky would have his own words for everything. He would call a vest a 'Shift.' He would always have his cap on, even in the bath and when he was getting shaved. He said he never felt dressed without it.

Dave Ditchburn

Moffet Sreet Fish And Chip Shop

When my father Albert Wilkinson started the fish and chip shop in Moffet Street with my mother Catherine, he was still recovering from a motor bike accident and was walking on two sticks. One Christmas they missed the last bus home. It was snowing and lying four or five inches thick and they had to walk from Westoe to Marsden. It was a hell of a walk for my dad and that was when they decided to get the first van, the Standard Eight, CU7 776.

The hours were six days a week, but on Friday and Saturday there were two openings. He got up at six o'clock and by half past he would be on his way to the shop to pick up the empty boxes from the day before and the swill and the heads and tails of the fish that had been gutted. Then he would get the quarter to seven ferry, the old *Northumbria*, over to North Shields. He would sell the swill at the quay. It used to go to the pig farmers. He would get a ticket for it which he saved up and cashed in once a year for a bit extra holiday money. He would get on the

Moffet Street fish and chip shop, 1983.

The wedding reception of Catherine Freeman and Albert Wilkinson on 8 January 1945. On the left is the best man, Robert Nicholson, on the right is Margaret Freeman, sister of the bride.

fish quay just before seven to have a look and see what was what. There would be cod, haddock, skate, flatties and the odd shark which would be shipped down south for steaks. The bell would ring at seven and the buying and selling started. Across the quay stretched a hundred and fifty yards of fish boxes and we had to stand on them to walk the length of the quay and choose the stock. Blokes in white coats and wellingtons walked around selling fish. If you bought a box, or a line of boxes, you had little name tags to identify them. You had to keep an eye on your boxes though. You've always got the element of roguery. If they weren't straight in the van, they would go.

We used to do daft things when we

had a spare moment. There was an old boy who used to hang around the quay trying to pick fish up cheap. He wandered around with bundles of papers under his arm and every now and again someone would set fire to them and there would be flames and smoke blasting out behind him. We would attach crabs or a lobster to his coat and you would see it hanging off his coat with its nipper swinging for his backside.

Each day the shop would average about twelve boxes of fish. I could just manage to lift a box. Sweet William, which is dogfish, has three names – Sweet William, Rock Salmon and Dogfish. But if you're a Mackum, its 'Woof'. We had to strip the skin off it and cut off the fins as well because there was a poisonous spike in the dorsal. If you got a jab it was like a bee sting. Then we would get the pliers to rip its skin of in one go.

We used to do fish and chips for all sorts of places. When we put them in the van the windows would steam up so much you couldn't see where you were going.

That back shop was freezing. When I left school I worked there for six weeks, but I had to pack in because my fingers stung with the cold. It was like getting the stick at school. A woman called Vi used to cut the potatoes into chips by hand. She started in the shop about seven and she used to have to fill four big wooden barrels with chips every day. She had a hell of a job. The water would have whitening in it to keep the chips fresh. She used to peel and eye the potatoes by hand in winter and in summer. She used to give my dad a hand to mix the batter in a big bucket. He had a special mix with coconut oil.

Raymond Wilkinson

For us kids, the fish and chip shop on the corner of Marshall Wallis Road was a collecting place because it was always open when the other shops were closed and on a dark night it was like a beacon to us. We would take it in turns to buy a four pence bag of chips and they would keep us going throughout the night.

Malcolm Grady

Victoria Road Landsale Coal Depot. (Courtesy Beamish Muaseum)

Model Trains

Dr Ord used to have a surgery opposite the Regent cinema at Westoe and he was a big fan of model trains. He had a big model railway in his house with huge amounts of tracks and trains and he was quite famous for it in the town.

Hugh Amess

Westoe Village

My parents were married in 1920 and they set up house in Osborne Avenue. At that time Westoe was regarded as the centre of Shields. There was a pond at the end of the village where the conveniences were. Most of the houses around the village were built for the ship owners like Brigham and Cowan.

Edith Atkinson

Where the college is now at Westoe was a farm. The farmer, a big stout bloke, used to go around Westoe with his horse and milk cart and we bought the milk out of a big churn. We never bought milk at the shops.

Jean Cockayne

One of my mother's favourite spare time occupations was walking around the elegant houses in Westoe Village. When you passed some of the houses you could quite often hear music being played inside. At the top of Blagdon Avenue, the first houses to be built didn't have bathrooms. By the

Edith Atkinson, with her older sister Joan, in Osborne Avenue in the 1930s.

The Man With The Rattle

There was an ex-miner who was a bit 'not with it', and he went around John Clay Street, Ada Street, George Potts Street and Stevenson Street with a football rattle shouting, 'There will be a meeting in the Marsden Miners' Hall in Imeary Street at 7.30 tonight!' There wasn't you know. In the beginning people use to turn up to the hall and then they gradually cottoned on to what was happening.

Ernie Keedy

Mr Chuter Ede after winning South Shields for Labour in 1929. PC Joseph Armstrong is on the left. (Photo Shields Gazette.)

time they built ours at number fifty six, they were installing bathrooms. They put them in the rest later.

Jean Shanahan

On Sunday evenings we would walk across the fields at Westoe to Hemsley's farm house and call in and get a glass of milk each. It was straight from the cow and nice and warm.

Tom Dawson

PC Joseph Armstrong

Before the war started my dad, Police Constable Joseph Armstrong, was seconded to the ARP and he gave a lot of lectures around the town about air raid precautions. During the war he was based at the Regent garage which was next to the Regent cinema. The property belonged to Pratt and he also had an office downstairs on the Imeary Street side in what became Westoe Florists. If there was a raid on he always had to go down there in case the town was badly blitzed and he could start up the distribution of blankets and gas masks. At one o'clock in the morning of 24 May 1943 he was siting in the office. For some reason he decided to have a word with one of the wardens who was in the office right outside the cinema. Then the bombs started falling on Stevenson Street, Cadwell and then Westoe. Then one came down right beside the cinema and along with a lot of people he was killed that night. That was the very last air raid on the town and he was one of the few of policemen killed in the town. Miss Flag, the local historian, was a regular visitor to his office. She took photographs of the bomb damage. Until she died she used to bring us a bunch of Lilly of the Valley out of her own garden each year on the anniversary of his death. In 1947 my mother opened a shop right opposite to where his office was and she managed to run the business by her self and bring up three kids

Shiela Burrows

Harton Village

I remember the old blacksmith's shop beside The Ship pub. Then later the place became Coulson's Taxis. Stamp's sweet shop was on the corner and it had a big bulls eye window in the front and you could see the sweets inside. Woodie's Farm was just across the road from the shop. There was also a big old house next to the High School which used to be the Hind's house. They were farmers as well. Ozzy Hind was electrocuted while he was ploughing a field near Centenary Avenue. Lightning struck the plough and it went right

In the Wintergardens at the Nook, 1950. Included are: Bill Salkeld, Ralph McDermott and Mary Gill.

through him and it also killed the two horses. He survived, but he was paralysed and had a stroke.

Bill Salkeld

Uncle Jack and Aunt Belle

My Uncle Jack and his wife, Aunt Belle, lived in the Aged Miners' homes off Marsden Road. When we visited, he would be sitting in a rocking chair beside the black leaded fireplace. The fire would be blazing away and he would be dressed in a collarless shirt, dark jacket and trousers, and there would be an embroidered smoking cap on his bald head. Beside his chair would be a walking stick and a spittoon because, like many miners, coal dust had settled in his lungs and he was constantly coughing and spitting to try to clear them. Jack and Belle had been together for fifty years but they were opposites in many ways. He was quick tempered, round shouldered and he talked very little. She was placid, stood straight and had rosy cheeks and talked a lot. As we went inside the bungalow Aunt Belle would be standing at the kitchen door wearing a long white dress and a sparkling white pinafore and her grey hair would be arranged into a bun, high on the back of her head. He would only turn in his chair and nod. They had no children so Belle devoted herself to Uncle Jack. She once told us that when he was working she would have a meal made for him when he came home and quiet words ready in case work had gone badly that day. But if his anger was too strong he would find fault with his meal, grab the plate and throw the

Great Uncle Jack Corner in Marsden Road Aged Miners' homes.

whole lot into the fire and storm off into the garden. I think she must have shed a few quiet tears for that man.

Ken Corner

The Hut

I used to have to go to the hut on Horsley Hill field that served that area until the shops were built. It stood where the church is now. There was a plank leading up to it across the field, so in the wet weather people didn't have to get their feet soaking. There were two council houses around there as well and I think they were used as grocery shops.

Mary Peterson

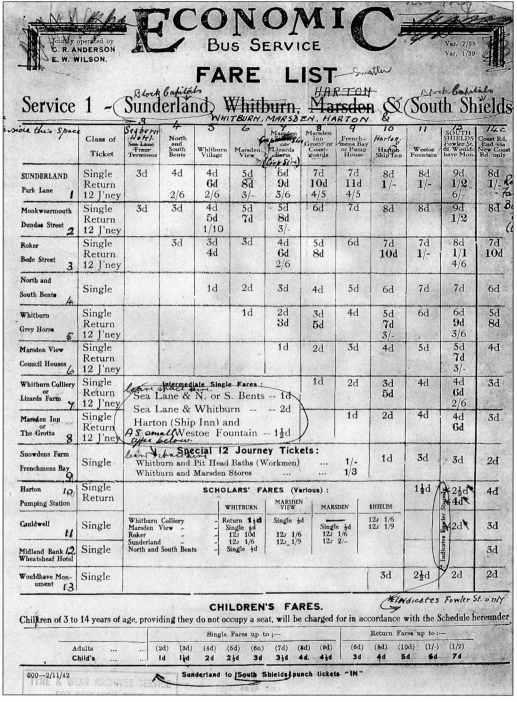

ECONOMIC BUS SERVICE

Jointly operated by
C. R. ANDERSON
E. W. WILSON.

Var. 7/38
Var. 1/39

FARE LIST

Service 1 – Sunderland, Whitburn, Marsden & South Shields

Class of Ticket	Seaburn Hotel Sea Lane Tram Terminus	North and South Bents	Whitburn Village	Marsden View	Marsden Grotto or Lizards Farm	Marsden Inn Grotto or Coastguards	French-mens Bay or Pump House	Harton Ship Inn	Westoe Fountain	SOUTH SHIELDS Fowler St. & Wouldhave Mon.	Coast Rd. End via New Coast Rd. only
SUNDERLAND Park Lane 1 Single	3d	4d	4d	5d	6d	7d	7d	8d	8d	9d	8d
Return			6d	8d	9d	10d	11d	1/-	1/-	1/2	1/-
12 J'ney		2/6	2/6	3/-	3/6	4/5	4/5			6/-	
Monkwearmouth Dundas Street 2 Single	3d	3d	4d	5d	5d	6d	7d	8d	8d	9d	8d
Return			5d	7d	8d					1/2	
12 J'ney			1/10		3/-						
Roker Bede Street 3 Single		3d	3d	3d	4d	5d	6d	7d	7d	8d	7d
Return			4d		6d	8d		10d	1/-	1/1	10d
12 J'ney					2/6					4/6	
North and South Bents 4 Single			1d	2d	3d	4d	5d	6d	7d	7d	6d
Whitburn Grey Horse 5 Single				1d	2d	3d	4d	5d	6d	6d	5d
Return					3d	5d		7d		9d	8d
12 J'ney								3/-		3/6	
Marsden View Council Houses 6 Single					1d	2d	3d	4d	5d	5d	4d
Return										7d	
12 J'ney										3/-	
Whitburn Colliery or Lizards Farm 7 Single						1d	2d	3d	4d	4d	3d
Return								5d		6d	
12 J'ney										2/6	
Marsden Inn or The Grotto 8 Single							1d	2d	4d	4d	3d
Return										6d	
12 J'ney											
Snowdens Farm Frenchmens Bay 9 Single								1d	3d	3d	2d
Harton Pumping Station 10 Single									1½d	2½d	4d
Return										4d	
Cauldwell 11 Single										2½d	3d
Midland Bank Wheatsheaf Hotel 12 Single											3d
Wouldhave Monument 13 Single								3d	2½d	2d	2d

Intermediate Single Fares:
Sea Lane & N. or S. Bents — 1d
Sea Lane & Whitburn — — 2d
Harton (Ship Inn) and Westoe Fountain — 1½d

Special 12 Journey Tickets:
Whitburn and Pit Head Baths (Workmen) … 1/-
Whitburn and Marsden Stores … … 1/3

SCHOLARS' FARES (Various):

	WHITBURN	MARSDEN VIEW	MARSDEN	SHIELDS
Whitburn Colliery Marsden View Roker	Return 1½d Single ½d 12s 10d	Single ½d 12s 1/6	Single ½d 12s 1/6	12s 1/6 12s 1/9
Sunderland North and South Bents	Single ½d 12s 1/6	12s 1/6	12s 2/-	

*Indicates Fowler St. only

CHILDREN'S FARES.

Children of 3 to 14 years of age, providing they do not occupy a seat, will be charged for in accordance with the Schedule hereunder.

		Single Fares up to :—								Return Fares up to :—				
Adults	(2d)	(3d)	(4d)	(5d)	(6d)	(7d)	(8d)	(9d)		(6d)	(8d)	(10d)	(1/-)	(1/2)
Child's	1d	1½d	2d	2½d	3d	3½d	4d	4½d		3d	4d	5d	6d	7d

300—2/11/42

Sunderland to South Shields punch tickets "IN"

An early draft of an Economic bus timetable.

Travel Economic

Wilson and Anderson ran the Economic Bus service between Sunderland and South Shields via Horsley Hill. The Economic was allowed to exist as a buffer between the council services and the Northern. Each company wouldn't let the other buy the Economic out. Neither of them wanted the coast road route because at that time it wasn't very profitable. Years after roll ticket machines were invented, the Economic company kept on using the old single tickets and the drivers would carry them around in a wooden ticket holder.

John Tinmouth

Dirty Smoke And Steam

In the late 1960s the 50-51 bus service ran from Whiteleas over the John Reid Road roundabout and then down Boldon Lane to Stanhope Road. Running roughly parallel was the old Sunderland to South Shields railway line. The pits were still churning out millions of tons of coal and the lines were full of coal trains. If you were fortunate enough you would get a train running the route at the same time as the bus. The trains were coal hoppers and mainly pulled by dirty, unkempt and full of character ex LNER freight engines and they travelled very slowly. As my bus came to the top of the Whiteleas estate, I saw a pall of dirty smoke above the houses and there it was, a freight engine. As the bus went down Boldon Lane I was craning my head around trying to keep the engine in view as it passed behind the signal box and over the level crossing. Then the bus stopped at the Victoria (Windscales) pub to pick up passengers and the train pulled out of sight. Then we were off again and I could glimpse it between the cuts and the street ends of the houses on Boldon Lane. Then the bus got caught up at the corner of Boldon Lane and Stanhope Road and I could just glimpse the train going over the bridge at Tyne Dock, what a magnificent sight it made. Then the bus pulled away down Stanhope Road and I was left with a hell of a crick in my neck from trying to follow the fast disappearing spout of dirty steam and smoke. That was thirty years ago and I'll never forget it.

Eddy Post

You Haven't Changed A Thing

We've had some famous people in our shop. Jimmy Saville often popped in when he was visiting relatives in the town. I think he came partly because of the ice cream and coffee but also because he comes from Scarborough and he knows the Scarborough branch of our family. For years people have always been coming into the shop in Ocean Road and telling us, 'You haven't changed a thing.' Well we have! Almost everything has been replaced but we've just kept to the original style.

Michael Minchella

The pier approach in the late 1920s. Although the general view is still recognisable, almost all of the features have now been swept away. (Courtesy Beamish Museum)

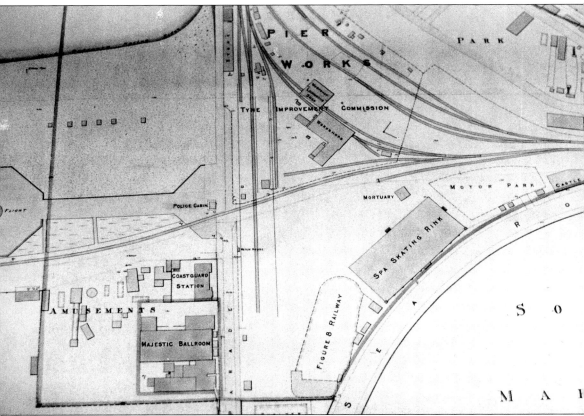

A Tyne Improvement Commission map (1934) of the area around the pier blockyard shows just how much has changed. Note the existence of a mortuary near the skating rink. (Tyne and Wear Archives)

CHAPTER 6

Leisure and Special Occasions

South Shields AFC, 1922-23. (Courtesy Beamish Museum)

The North Beach around 1925. (Courtesy South Tyneside Libraries)

What A Nice Man!

Until after the war we had never really been on holiday. When we came home from our first break the porter at the station helped us off with all our bags and cases and we just said, 'Thank you very much', and walked off. We didn't realise you had to tip porters, it never entered our heads. We didn't know anything about tipping.

Mary Peterson

I used to know a lot of people who came from down south to Shields for their holidays. They all used to think it was great and wouldn't hear a bad word said about the town.

Jean Shanahan

Beach Tents

We used to take our own food down to the beach to one of the wooden huts. My grandmother had a stall at the beach and she used to do really well selling hot water.

Jean Cockayne

People went down to the beach at Easter to clean their tent out. My aunt's had a sideboard and chairs inside and my father used to say she had better crockery down at the beach than she had in the house. By the summer everyone had their things spread out outside their tent in a half circle and when we were walking along the beach we didn't dare trespass into anyone else's space. There would be groups of people siting outside of their tents and there would be the smell of hot tea and cucumber sandwiches and the sound of people gossiping to each other. Mind you, that was the posh end and we were never down there. We used to get our Niels pram out, put our tent on it and then fill it full of bottles of milk and things. Then we would walk down through Westoe Village and through the allotments. There was a little house on the Leas called The Nest, they had a little tea garden out the back and they would sell us hot water. There was no road then, just a little track and one of us had to hold the front of the pram to get it down to the beach.

Olga Carlson

Along The Prom

We used to take a clothes horse and a blanket down to the beach to build a tent. That was when there used to be a six foot drop from the promenade to the beach. The prom was built by people who were on means tested work schemes and I think that was why it was so horrible and not artistic at all.

Ernie Keedy

The adventurous lads used to jump from the promenade down to the beach.

Olga Carlson

Shops in the North Marine Park at the base of the Law Top. (Courtesy South Tyneside Libraries)

Dance On The Sands.

Everyone went to the beach fully dressed. The men had their suits on, youngsters would have woollen gansey jumpers and grandma would be wearing her hat and a fur wrapped around her neck, even though it was the height of summer. Our family had a tent on the beach. It was home made and contained a set of draws, a table and a primus stove for boiling kettles and frying up food. Many people slept in the tents overnight, although that was frowned on by the council. In those days, the sand was about ten feet below the promenade and there were concrete aprons leading down to the beach. If someone brought a gramophone we would have a dance on the sands. The men would wear white shirts and very baggy pants called Oxford Bags. The girls would be in short dresses, or if they were very daring, a pair of beach pyjamas. They were considered daring by older people. At the fair there was the figure eight for tuppence a time and wooden ramshackle huts, that had been built just before the First World War, served as cafes. In the 1930s the Corporation had civic week in the South Marine Park. Everyone would go because it was something to relieve the pressures, especially if you were out of work. Amateur players would put on plays in the park and the bandstand would be illuminated with fairy lights.

John Landells

Before the war they would bring a wooden platform on to the beach, around Gandie's Temple, and people would have tea dances on there. I think that's why they call South Shields people 'Sand Dancers'.

Tom Dawson

The promenade in the 1930s. Elsie Wilson, mother of Edith Atkinson, with her cousin Emma Richards.

The bandstand in the South Marine Park in the early 1930s. Left to right: Edith Atkinson (nee Wilson), sister Joan, mother Elsie and Emma Richards.

In the summer there would always be a band playing in the park and we would dance around the bandstand. They used to put some white powder on the ground so you could dance easier.

Jean Cockayne

Marsden Grotto

The steps down to Marsden Grotto used to move as you walked down because they were suspended on rope and you had to be careful of the overhanging limestone rocks.

Olga Carlson

When we were going down to the beech in the lift at Marsden Grotto the shaft used to be open and we got a great view of the beach through the little window in the lift door. I can remember being on the beach and seeing the workmen busily encasing the shaft with stone and thinking, well, that's that bit of fun spoilt!

Jerimia Cornelius

We used to have special clothes for Sunday. You where never allowed to wear them during the week unless it was a real special occasion. We had a marvellous time first footing at New Year. People would wander the streets till all hours in their best clothes. We would go around our relatives and at every house they would have a buffet.

Jean Cockayne

I started dancing at St Michael's church recreation rooms. We used to go to church dances because my parents, in particular my dad, were very strict. He used to say, 'You have to be in by such and such a time or I am out there looking for you.' I was allowed to go to the Hedworth Hall when I got a bit older. There they had a proper orchestra, it was great. Johnny Openshaw and his band also used to play there. We used to dance there every Saturday night. You couldn't get any alcohol, a cup of tea was the most we got, but we used to have a really good night there. Once, when I was dancing the Tango at the Hedworth, I was clutched very tightly to my partner

who was an idiot. I had my back to the band and when it stopped playing he let me go straight away and I fell right amongst the drums. Everyone laughed but I told him I didn't think it was very funny and stormed off.

Jean Cockayne

Extremely Strict

The Hedworth Ballroom had a lovely floor. The Majestic Ballroom was at the bottom of Ocean Road and there was the Crown halfway along Ocean Road. The Majestic was run by Mr Davies and you either behaved yourself or you were out. It was all strictly ballroom. There were times when you could do jive or the jitterbug and those times were very clearly announced. If

Marsden Grotto with open lift shaft.

An afternoon on the Leas beside Marsden grotto in 1949.

anyone did jive when they were playing a quickstep, they used to come up to you and say 'get off the floor'.

Ethel Dawson

Football

I used to play football for Laygate School as a junior and our arch enemies were Barnes Road School. We met in the league and the cup and we had some real battles. When we got to the grammar school some of us were playing on the same team and that was very interesting at first.

Malcolm Grady

If Its A Nice Day

In the summer we used to stand in Canterbury Street and point to Cleadon Chimney and say, 'If its a nice day tomorrow, we'll go up there and have a picnic'. We loaded the pram up with bread sandwiches and bottles of milk and pushed it up to the hills. We sat and ate our sandwiches with our backs against the big wall around the sanatorium.

Olga Carlson

The Ash Carnival

We used to get dressed up for the carnival in Shields. We would go to a warehouse containing fancy dress outfits and I would often pick out a gypsy outfit. We had an Airedale called Molly and we used to put a union jack across her back and fix two baskets to

113

Harton Colliery Band. South Shields

The Harton Colliery band originally known as the Tyne Dock Temperance Band. (Courtesy South Tyneside Libraries)

her and people would put money inside for charity. She collected quite a lot. The parade ended up on the spare ground behind Eldon Street called 'The Ash'. There would also be a fair there every year which stayed for a week. I loved to ride the shuggyboats, you could pay 2d and stay on as long as you liked. I would stay on for hours until the attendants threw me off.

Joyce Carlson

Billy Smarts Circus

The whole school at Laygate used to be let out to watch Billy Smarts Circus march through the town. They used to come up Laygate Lane to Chichester and then raise the tent at Brinkburn. We would all be leaning against the railings watching the elephants, wagons, clowns and stiltwalkers coming up the street.

Malcom Grady

South Shields Museum

In South Shields Museum in Ocean Road there was Wilson the ship owner's collection of wild animals, the model of the satellite, Captain Johnson's collection of ship models from Readheads, the sword from the South Shields Volunteers in the Napoleonic wars, little radios that were made in the Japanese concentration camps during the Second World War and loads of William Boyse's paintings.

John Tinmouith

Westoe Colliery Football Team, 1952-53. Included are: Terry Killen, Charles Carlson and Tom Killen.

Redheads Football Team, 1946-47. Included are: Alan Forest, A. Gallen, Tony Hawthorne, Jack Thorpe, Jackie Martin, Vincent Taylor.

The Bedlington Rudolph Valentino Jazz Band marching along Westoe Road. (Courtesy Beamish Museum)

A group of children in fancy dress passing H. Duffin's newsagents shop on Alexander Street. (Courtesy Beamish Museum)

CHAPTER 7

Stage and Screen

The Troubadours Concert Party, 1932. Included are: Fred Appleby, George Stevenson, George Swanson, Betty Wilkinson, Mr Shorey, Mrs Shorey, Sylvia Shorey and Arthur Appleby.

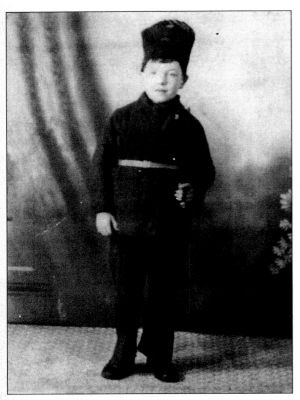

Bob Hedley (aged 8), the mascot of the South Shields Male Voice Choir.

Nine Pence For A Torch.

The very first time I ever trod on the stage and earned money was when I was seven. There was a theatre in South Shields called The Alexander and someone, I don't know who it was, entered me for a singing competition. I can remember the evening vividly. My brother Tom, who worked at Whitburn Pit, had said to me, 'If you win, I'll buy you a flashlight.' This was a torch I'd seen in Goldman's window on Ocean Road. It was nine pence. I didn't have the nine pence, nobody in the family had the money to spare. A girl called Emily Robson sang a song called, 'Little Pal' and I sang a song called 'No Mans Land' which was a very weepy thing about the First World War and it was always good for a round of applause. When they had selected everyone and put them to one side, there was Emily and I left on stage. The compare said, 'Right we've got to get on with the play, lets have a decision.' He put his hand on my head and I got a round of applause, then Emily's, and the applause was level. Then he said, 'We must have a decision, ladies and gentlemen, we must have a decision.' He put his head on Emily's head, thunderous applause, then he put his hand on my head and the theatre started rocking. It was a very small theatre, it had wooden seats and wooden balconies, and that theatre just rattled. The three half crowns were stuffed into my hand and I was ushered off the stage. My brother had been in the gallery with his friends from the pit and they had their pit boots on. They had hacked that front to bits to make enough noise to make sure I got that seven and six. To top it all, my brother actually had the torch all ready for me in a brown paper bag in his pocket.

Bob Hedley

'Troubadours Are Here Again'

The Troubadours concert party was run by my father, Isaac and my mother. They formed the party round about 1932 with Arthur Appleby who came to lodge with us. We went right round the north by lorry, giving shows at various halls. My earliest memories were of being carried home in this lorry late at night when I was around three-years-old, and being asleep on the way

The Troubadours Concert Party on stage. Included are: Ginger Pyle, Issac Wilkinson, Dolly Young, Jimmy Gilpin, Dolly Taws and Flora Taws.

and my father lifting me up and putting me over his shoulder. I was always very cold and I was just glad to get in the house and go to bed. There were about 20 to 25 people in the show and the ages varied from about ten upwards. The show opened to the tune of, 'Happy Days are here again' but the words they would sing would be, 'Troubadours are here again.' When the show closed they were all on the stage singing, 'It's time to say goodbye.' There was Ginger Pyle and one man called George Swanson who dressed up as a Chinese mandarin and his favourite performance was a monologue of the 'Green Eye of the Little Yellow God'. There was Jimmy Gilpin, my uncle, who later moved to Richmond and there was my mother's friend, Mrs Shorey, her husband and their daughter, and Mr and Mrs Taws. Their daughter, Flora, was one of the performers, she only died about five years ago.

Joyce Carlson

The Mirror Dance

We played at the Alexander Theatre in King Street and the

Flora Taws – The Mirror Dance.

show always had to be over at ten o'clock at night because that was the law of the land. When my daughter, Flora, came on stage there were gasps of admiration from the audience because the dress she wore was so beautiful. She would dance a dance called the mirror dance.

Dolly Taws

When I was five, the Troubadours performed a sketch at the Zion hall in Laygate called the slimming machine. Arthur Appleby was dressed as a doctor in a white coat, and he claimed that he had invented a machine which could reduce people's weight. It was a large wooden box about seven foot high and six by six feet with a door at either side. The first patient to go in was Dolly Young, she was quite overweight. The door was shut, Arthur turned a handle and there were screams from the patient. Backstage, two or three people whirled football rattles around and after about twenty seconds the door on the opposite side opened and a slightly slimmer member of the show walked out. She had the same clothes on but she was smaller, so they were hanging on her a bit. This was repeated two or three times and each time someone new came on, Arthur said, 'Oh no, she is not slim enough.' The last one out was my mother and when she went back in screams came from inside the machine, there was a loud bang on a drum and then a large cow thigh bone was thrown out with the dress on it. The dress was just a rag by this time and then the curtains came down. Well, I was sitting

The Zion Hall. Shortly after closing as a venue it became a Unemployed Social Centre. (Courtesy South Tyneside Libraries)

Kathleen Burdon on right.

the concert party and more or less calling her a traitor. Of course it was probably just jealousy.

The show broke up in 1939 because of the war. We all went into war work although George Swanson kept a show of his own going in Shields. There were often reports in the *Gazette* about it.

Joyce Carlson

An Elitist Thing

When I was eight some of the girls at school used to dance, but it was mostly tap dancing. There were very few ballet teachers in this part of the world and it was even considered to

Jack Burdon

in the audience with a friend of my parents and I thought I had seen my mother for the last time. I just screamed and in fact I went hysterical and the friend had to take me backstage to show me that my mother was really all right.

One time we had a bad audience in North Shields. They talked during the performance. I remember them (backstage) saying, 'Fancy they even talked during Dolly Young's song.' Dolly Young was considered a star singer. They all voted to walk out, packed their bags and left the audience sitting waiting for the second half to start.

One of the girls in the show sang a song called 'Blue Moments' and she got the chance to be in a show in London. I used to hear them talking about her in

122

be an elitist thing. I started off tap dancing at Jean Heilbron's class. Her father George Heilbron taught ballroom dancing. Jean ran a dancing school, it was a shilling a week and we went there every Saturday afternoon. I loved it. My brother Jack worked in Wiggs Music Shop in Ocean Road selling records, sheet music and pianos. He had a great love of classical music, and I was brought up on Benjamino Gigli. He used to call me in and say, 'Come and listen to the great maestro.' His influence made me love classical music and although he didn't do ballet, he brought me books out of the library with pictures of ballerinas and that was when I decided that ballet was what I wanted to do. I had my early training at Olga Bolton's ballet school in Sunderland Road opposite the Methodist church. She had the attic converted into a dance studio.

Kathleen Burdon

Treading The Boards

When I was eight I was the mascot of the South Shields Male Voice Choir. When I was nine I was in the concert party called The Familiar Artists doing a horrible impression of Will Fyffe with a cap, muffler and a clay pipe singing, 'I Belong to Glasgow'. There were South Shields comedians like Len Long, Jimmy Macavou and Ginger Pyle, all First World War men, who got paid only about half a crown to perform in theatres because there wasn't a lot of money going about. A concert party of five would share something like twelve shillings, maybe fifteen,

sometimes less, depending on where you worked. When I was twelve, the local licensing authority granted me a licence to appear in Cine-variety. The Queens Theatre was Cine-variety. It showed a film and during the interval you had a few acts, then they would revert back to the big picture again. I did that for a while at places like The Queens and The Villiars Theatre in South Shields. It was just a case of doing your two or three songs, applause, and then you were off and somebody else came on.

At St John's School I would have to tell the teacher in advance that I would be performing in a matinee. When it got towards the time I would get up and go. The other kids would look at me and the expression in their eyes would be, 'lucky dog', and I would go off to work at the theatre.

Bob Hedley

The Queens Theatre

I used to go to The Queens Theatre in Mile End Road with my mother and father. I thought the theatre was magical, but once we went to visit the dressing rooms and I was surprised how cold and shabby they were. Later on, when I started to paint, that image stayed with me and has recurred in some of my paintings.

Joyce Carlson

Arthur Mertz's Pierrots

In 1936 the pierrots on the sea front were run by a big fat jolly man called

Bob Hedley on stage with the Silver Songsters.

Arthur Mertz. In the troop was Ollie Popinger, Crofty Popinger and a pianist called Bobby Gill. When I joined them I was getting thirty-five bob a week, almost as much as my dad was getting at the pit. Arthur would parade up and down the promenade wearing an evening cape and a ridiculously small hat. The rest of the performers would be dressed up as slaves and they would be handing out leaflets for the evening performances and he would pretend to be urging them on with a cabby's whip. The stage was in the open, half on the promenade and half on the beach. The dressing rooms were underneath. The deck chairs at the front were six pence, the hard seats further back were three pence and there was a barrier at the back from which the non paying public could watch the show. Wednesday night would be crazy night with every audience participation stunt in the

book. We would give away light tin pots, pans and kettles, which Arthur used to buy for sixpence each at Woolworth's. Thursday was audience 'have a go' night where our patrons could perform for similar prizes.

When Staffani and his Silver Songsters came to The Queens in February 1936 I was taken down for an audition and told I had got the job half way through. On the Monday there were crowds of people at South Shields station waving their children off. It was quite exiting for me. The platform was full of theatre acts and big boxes containing scenery. On the tour we used to sell boxes of ten or twelve inch records inside the theatre. Two lads were sent into the auditorium, two to the stalls, one to the circle and one to the 'gods'. If you were sent to the 'gods' you had to carry those records right up and really earned your commission.

When we got home my dad asked me what I wanted to do now because I was out of a job. I said I would like to go down the pit. He didn't say anything. He just threw a boot at me. He said, 'You'll get another theatre job and in the meantime I'll give you half a crown a week.' Well, I knew the lads at The Regent – Joe Cable, the chief projectionist was killed at Dunkirk. They took me under their wing, let me load films and wind projectors. In those days The Regent was part of the Shepherd Consortium along with the Picture House, The Regent, The Pavilion and The Palladium where the store is at the Nook. A vacancy occurred at the Picture House in Ocean Road for a rewind boy. It was known to the locals as 'The Cozey'. I was told, 'Robin get yourself down quick, see Mr Kenny.' He asked what experience I had and I told him and he told me to start on Monday. I was there until the war.

Bob Hedley

The Tivoli Theatre

Children could pay to get into the Tivoli Theatre with jam jars rather than money. If you gave them a two pound jar or two one pound jars, you were in. When we got in we were given a comic and told to sit on the floor. There was someone there with a big stick to hit the bairns with if they became unruly. The Grand Electric was the first picture house in Shields to have talkies. They weren't films, they were shorts and there was a fellow called Teddy Brown who played a zilaerphone. The Pavilion was always presumed to

have the best acoustics though.

Ernie Keedy

Avoid The Usherettes

If they could avoid the usherettes, some people would sit thorough the same picture four times. Not because they wanted to see it four times but because the cinema was always a cosy warm place and they didn't have the money to heat their own homes properly in the winter.

John Landells

A painting by Joyce Carlson inspired by the backstage of the Queen's Theatre.

125

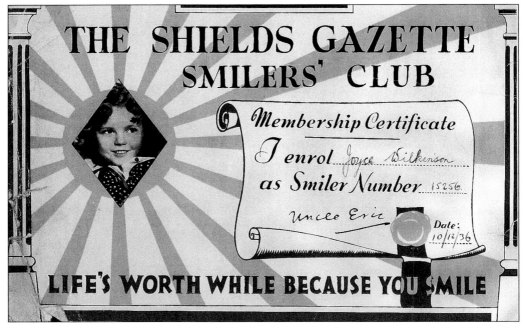

THE SHIELDS GAZETTE
SMILERS' CLUB

Membership Certificate
I enrol *Joyce Wilkinson*
as Smiler Number *15256*

Uncle Eric

Date:
10/12/36

LIFE'S WORTH WHILE BECAUSE YOU SMILE

Shields Gazette Smilers' Club certificate. Many South Shields children joined this popular club in the 1930s, inspired by Shirley Temple.

The Bobby Thompson Talent Competition at the Pier Pavilion in 1952. Left to right: Christine Colman, unknown, Bobby Thompson, Jean Henderson and Hugh Slater.

126

Feet Up!

At The Palladium cinema there use to be a man called One Armed Peter who used to come around and spray you with Flit to get rid of the fleas.

We also used to go to the old Westoe cinema in Chichester Road, known as the Chi, for the children's films. There was no upstairs or down stairs but just a continuous rising ramp of seats from bottom to top. Right at the top were the toilets and they were really primitive. Often with all the kids using them they would overflow and it would all start running out of the toilets and down the sloping floor. When that happened, up would go the cry, 'Feet up, feet up!'

Tom Dawson

Quite often we would be at the cinema and the screen would suddenly darken. If they needed to get the attention of someone in the audience, they would write a message on a slide then push it into a special slot in the projector. A message would appear saying would Mrs So and So report to the manager's office.

Bob Hedley

Teenage Delinquents

When we started out we were a skiffle group called The Teenage Delinquents. Our first gigs were at Tyne Dock youth club and then at the pie and peas suppers at the Dean Road over sixties centre. When we were fourteen and playing pub gigs we couldn't have a drink, but the landlord would sometimes let us have a half between us on condition that we stood in the cellar to drink it.

Dave Ditchburn

Snapping And Fighting

I joined the amateur dramatics after Tom, my husband, died. They were all full of themselves. When the results of the auditions went up they were always saying to each other, 'How did she get that part, how did he get that.' Not that they used to talk about me because I was nothing. In the dressing rooms they were always snapping and fighting with each other all the time the show was on. They would throw your costume off the racks to get theirs and wouldn't pick yours up if it went on the floor. In the wings they would push and shove each other, then they would run on stage and it would be all songs and smiles.

Mary Peterson

Pontop Pike

My father didn't drink and that was how we were able to afford a television set for the Coronation in 1953. The service from Pontop Pike was just about to start and he went to Holdsworth's in Dean Road and paid ninety pounds for a set with a fourteen inch screen. On the day of the Coronation we had twenty-seven people in our living room at Bewick Street. My mother made them cups of tea but they all brought their own sandwiches because she wanted to see the

Bob Hedley on stage during 'Miss Tyne Tees'.

Coronation as well.

Joyce Carlson

Our first TV was called a white eye. The case was white and bevelled and the set had a twelve inch screen. After the aeriel was fitted I noticed that people walking up our road crossed to the other side before they reached our house. They thought they were going to be struck down by invisible rays.

Olga Carlson

I worked as a television repair man for several years in the 1950s. One winter I was called to this chap's house to make a repair. The whole of the ground floor was empty except for the cooker, a chair and this big expensive TV set. Several of the floorboards were missing and one was resting half in the fire and half on a chair so as it burned down it would feed into the fire. I think he had sold off almost everything to buy the TV set.

Harry Peasland

Wacky Jacky

I got a job on the *One O'Clock Show* while the studios at Tyne Tees Television were being finished off. I sent a series of sketches to George Black who ran the place with Alfred Black. George was more severe than Alfred. Alfred was the gent but the real dynamo was George. He was always racing around checking on production. I was working with Terry O'Neil, Austin Steel, Len Martin, George Romaine, Chris Langford and Billy Hutchinson. The show ran for eleven years and I wrote some of the 'Wacky Jacky' scripts but I didn't get anything extra for that. If I had been at the BBC, I would be in a bigger house by now. We eventually did one thousand and ninety-six *One O'Clock Shows*. Eventually I left to join the BBC in London. I was on *Crackerjack* for seven years. I was writing little sketches and nonsense for kids, it was beautiful. You got rid of all your old gags that way. The kids love them. I still do some of them now in shows in Shields and they always ask, 'Where did you get that one from?'

Bob Hedley